# WAR

Isabel Lucero

WAR



Cover Design:
Robin Harper from Wicked by Design

Interior Design and Formatting by:
Christine Borgford from Perfectly Publishable

# CHAPTER 1

"WHAT THE FUCK DO YOU think you're doing?" I shout as soon as we're in the car. "Are you trying to get yourself killed?"

"Hell no, but I ain't about to let anybody step to me like he did. Is he out of his fucking mind?"

"I think you're out of your mind for pulling your gun out in the middle of the fucking street! Cops could have been watching, and you know PJ had a gun on him. He always does."

I press hard on the gas and speed down the road, heading towards our house.

"Fuck the cops and fuck PJ. I don't give a fuck about either."

"That's your problem, you don't give a fuck about anything. I don't care if you don't give a fuck about yourself, but when you put us all in danger, then it's my problem."

"Come on, C," he grumbles.

I ignore Jasper the rest of the way, because he already knows he's in the wrong. With everything that's going on, he pulls a gun out on someone in the middle of the street in broad fucking daylight. Idiot. And it wasn't just anyone he pulled a gun on, he had to threaten a guy who's part of Roman Rios' crew. Roman is a monster and he's training his crew to be just like him.

Not that my team isn't full of fucking criminal, ruthless bastards, but Roman will slit your throat in front of anybody in the middle of the day, and walk away calmly, because he knows nobody's gonna rat on him. They'd be stupid to.

While it's my plan to get things back on track again, I can't have Jasper or anybody on my crew going around and threatening the guy who has it out for us already.

This is what happened. My father, Memphis Reed, was the leader of this group of misfits we have going on here. He was the boss, the man in charge of everything, and nobody crossed him. Ever. He was my whole world. He raised me when my whore of a mother took off and left the both of us.

We're a protection racket. We offer protection to people and/or businesses who require us to make sure nobody fucks with them and their shit. Sometimes it's violent, but oftentimes people know not to fuck with anybody who's under our protection. Our reputation precedes us and that's worked well for us and our clients thus far, but Roman has decided he wants to try his hand in racketeering.

That wouldn't be a problem if he wasn't in our territory. We never had a problem with him selling drugs, weapons, extorting people, and whatever the fuck else he does around here, but there can't be two racketeering groups in the same area.

Let's say our client is going against their client and vying for a piece of land, or a particular building for their business. It's now on us to fight the other racketeers in order to secure the win for our respective clients. We can't offer a guarantee in that case, and if we lose, it leaves our client's protection unreliable and our services of very little value. Then soon enough, we aren't needed by anyone.

We cannot tolerate competition.

That's the situation we're in now, and it's becoming a big problem. They're trying to push us out so they can takeover, but I'm not leaving. I refuse to be bullied out of something my father spent his whole life building.

I pull into our lot and slam the car door behind me, storming into the house.

"Hey, C!"

"Chelle, what's goin' on, girl?"

I jet past Gage and Silas, making my way to the kitchen to grab a bottle of Jack. When I walk back into the living room they're both looking at me with wide eyes, and then Jasper walks in.

"What the fuck did you do to get her all pissed off?" Gage asks, pinning Jasper with a stare.

Jasper doesn't answer, he just walks up the stairs to his room. I fall onto the couch in between Gage and Silas and take a swig from the bottle.

"That bad?" Silas asks, swiping the bottle from me and taking a drink.

"Jasper pulled a gun out on PJ in the middle of the street."

"Roman's PJ?' Silas asks.

"You know any other PJ?' Gage snaps.

"Shut up. So, what happened?"

I steal the bottle back and take another drink. "Nothing . . . yet. PJ's gonna tell Roman about their fight. Jasper was running his mouth and talkin' like we ain't scared of them, and we're ready whenever they are and some other bullshit."

"Well, we ain't scared of them!" Gage shouts. "Fuck them. They know goddamn well what they're doing is wrong."

"I know, but we need a solid plan in place. We can't

go around pissing off his people and think everything's gonna be okay."

Gage strokes his beard like he's thinking about something. Silas takes the Jack from my hand and gulps it.

Gage has been around the longest and has always been like a brother to me. He also helps me run this organization. I don't know what I'd do without him. He's five years older than me at thirty-one, and definitely acts the roll of big brother. I appreciate the fact that he's there to protect me, but a lot of the time I don't need anybody to protect me. I can protect myself, something I have my dad to thank for, but Gage is also there to scare away any potential boyfriends. Not that I have any. Guys seem to be intimidated by me.

Maybe it's the tattoos. I have a chest piece that extends to my shoulders and down both arms. I always get people saying, "why did you ruin your body with all that ink?" or "you're so pretty, why all the tattoos?" Maybe because I do what the fuck I want. God, I hate judgmental people.

Then again, they might be intimidated by the fact that I have all these large, tattooed, scary looking guys around me all the time. Maybe it's because they know I carry a gun with me everywhere I go. Maybe it's because I can give a sailor a run for his money when it comes to cussing. Whatever it is, I don't have many prospects banging my door down.

Me, Jasper, Silas, and Gage all live in this house together. It's a large home with six bedrooms, four baths, and lots of space. Nothing too fancy, just spacious. We have a gate that closes in the whole lot, and we have another building behind the house that offers more privacy with clients. Our other crew members live elsewhere, but stop by enough that you'd think they lived here.

Silas puts his arm over my shoulder and squeezes me

into him. "We'll figure something out. Don't you worry your pretty little head about it."

"Thanks, Si," I respond, pulling out from his grasp.

Silas is big. Huge, actually. He stands at six-five and weighs well over two hundred pounds. Probably close to two-fifty, but I don't ask. He's got muscle, but it's not pure muscle. He's a few years older than me at twenty-nine, and he and Gage look like they could be brothers. They both have dark hair that's worn similarly; short on the sides, long on the top, and both have fairly long beards. I figure these guys hate that I'm in charge because I'm younger than them, but they don't say anything. My father put me in this place, and they respect that.

I stand up and take the Jack back to the kitchen. As I'm closing the cabinet, I hear the front door swing open.

"Where's Chevelley?"

"I'm here," I say, coming around the corner.

C, Chevelley, and Chelle. All the names the guys call me. There have been times I've wished my name was something simpler, but my dad named me, and I can definitely say I haven't heard of another Chevelley before.

Deacon stands there with a somewhat worried look on his face. "Roman got wind of some shit that went down not too long ago. Something with Jasper?" he questions.

I nod and wait for him to continue.

"I heard he's sending someone to come over here. Check things out."

"What the fuck does that mean? Check things out," Gage roars.

Gage and Deacon are around the same height at about five-eleven or so, but Gage has more mass to his body than Deacon. Deac has more of a swimmer's body while Gage has more of a football player's body. They're both equally tatted, but Deacon's tattoos extend up his neck and down his fingers, while Gage's tattoos can be hidden if he wears a long sleeved shirt.

"It means he's sending someone over here to talk to Chelle and make sure she's got things under control."

"PJ is the one who initiated contact with us today. Jasper blew up, but we weren't out looking for them," I state. "Why does he need to make sure my shit's under control? He's still fucking with our business."

Deacon sits on the chair and plops his booted feet onto the already scuffed coffee table. "I figured you'd want to know that you have a visitor on the way."

"Is he really acting like if my people don't talk to his people, that everything will be fine? We both can't be doing the same thing in the same area. He's fucking crazy."

"Look, C. There's something else you need to know." I don't respond. I just wait. "He's sending Xavier over."

My breath falters.

Xavier.

Xavier fucking Delgado.

Roman's number two.

He's twisted. He's vicious. He's terrifying.

And once upon a time, I thought I loved him.

Fuck.

# CHAPTER 2

"XAVIER'S COMING HERE?" I ASK, trying to sound unaffected.

"Yep," Deacon replies, pulling a pack of cigarettes from his pocket.

Gage quickly looks at me. "Can you handle this?"

I scowl at him. "Of course I can fucking handle this! What're you trying to say?"

"I'm not saying anything," Gage states. "I know your history with him, don't forget that."

Si turns around and looks at me. "We're here with you, C. Don't worry about that cocksucker."

"I'm not worried about Xavier, and there is no history," I say, making sure to look them all in the eye. "He's a fucking asshole, and we all know it. I was young and dumb once upon a time. I know better now. Okay?"

None of them respond vocally, and that just pisses me off, but it's not worth fighting about. I stalk over towards Deacon and steal a cigarette from his pack and storm outside.

"I'll be out front."

When I get outside, I pull the lighter from the front pocket of my shorts and light up the cigarette. Gage's black truck is parked out front, so I pull down the tailgate and sit down, waiting for Xavier to show up.

Fucking Xavier.

I met him when I was seventeen. He wasn't working for Roman at the time, but he was still living the same lifestyle we were. He was the bad boy every girl is drawn to, because he's everything your father wouldn't want you to be mixed up with. My dad, however, has always had these kinds of guys around me, but he trusted them. Well, he actually put the fear of God into them. They always knew I was off limits, but Xavier . . . Xavier didn't care what my dad said, and of course that made me like him even more. Stupid.

For the longest time, I just watched him. Not in a stalker kind of way, but if we were in the same location, my eyes followed him wherever he went. Girls of all ages flocked to him. He's six years older than me, so at that time, he was twenty-three. I was sure he had no idea who I was, after all, I was just a seventeen year old girl.

One day—a week before my eighteenth birthday—me, Gage, Deacon, Trax, and Jai were all hanging out at Jai's house. He was having some party, a party my dad let me go to because he knew Gage was going to watch out for me.

***Past***

*I'm in the kitchen smoking some weed with my friend Levi when the front door opens.*

*"Hey, X!" Jai yells over the music.*

*"What's going on, guys?" X replies. His voice is smooth, confident, and sexy.*

*"Who the hell is that?" Levi whispers.*

*"Xavier."*

*"Damn. I want to eat me some Xavier."*

*"Lee!" I squeal.*

*"Do you know him?" she asks.*

*"Not really. I know of him. I've seen him around a lot, but we don't talk or anything."*

*Lee and I watch Xavier and his friends move around the living room, talking to the other guys. Xavier's wearing jeans, black motorcycle boots, and a black leather jacket over his black T-shirt. Fuck. His hair is long on the top, falling over his forehead from time to time, and his facial hair proves he's all man.*

*"Let's take a shot," Lee whispers, already moving towards the liquor.*

*"If Gage catches me, I'm dead."*

*"He knows you're smoking weed," she replies with an eye roll.*

*"I know, but he's weird."*

*"We'll be quick."*

*She quickly pours two shots and we drink them down fast, rinse the glasses out, and put them back. We're both looking in the fridge, trying to find something to drink to mask the alcohol smell when we hear footsteps in the kitchen.*

*"What're you girls doing?"*

*Xavier's slightly Mexican-accented voice pours over me, drowning me in his sexiness. Lee and I quickly turn and stare at him.*

*"Nothing," we both answer together.*

*He smirks. "I think you're lying."*

*Lee pinches me on my thigh behind the fridge door, but I don't know what she's trying to tell me by doing that.*

*"We're just looking for something to drink," I say defensively.*

*His eyes move over towards the bottle of the liquor that's sitting next to the sink. Lee pinches me again, and now I realize we never put the liquor back where it was.*

*"I happen to know Jai keeps his liquor over there," he gestures to the section of the counter that holds all of Jai's liquor bottles.*

*Panicking, I say, "Please don't tell Gage. He'll kill me."*

*Xavier chuckles and then walks towards us. He stops right in front of me, the fridge door is the only thing between us.*

*"I can keep a secret."*

*His voice drips with sin.*

*Lee looks between us, and must notice that his eyes haven't moved from mine. She steps away from me and disappears into the living room.*

*Xavier's honey brown eyes are intense and I can't seem to pull my gaze from them. His mouth twists up into a lopsided smile.*

*"Don't worry, Chevelley. I won't say anything to Gage."*

*"You . . . you know my name?" I ask stupidly.*

*"Of course. You're Memphis' daughter."*

*I nod. "Yeah. That's me."*

*He leans over the door, grazing my leg as he reaches in for a beer. "How old are you, Chevelley?"*

*I think about lying and telling him I'm older than I am, but if he knows my name, my dad, and knows Gage, then I'm sure he either knows, or can find out soon.*

*"I'm almost eighteen."*

*"Almost?" he questions.*

*"In a week."*

*"Hmm." He pushes the hair that's fallen over his eyes back over his head. "Not old enough to drink, then."*

*"Old enough to do plenty," I reply bravely.*

*His eyebrow raises and then he takes a drink. "I'm old enough to get in trouble for giving you a taste."*

*My stomach flutters and my core tingles. He hands me his beer, but I know he's talking about me having a taste of something else other than his beer. I take the bottle and sip, never breaking eye contact. When I hand it back to him, he takes another drink.*

*"I'm sure I'll see you around," he says before turning around and going back into the living room.*

*As soon as he's gone, Lee comes barging in with wide eyes.*

*"Holy fuck! Did he kiss you? What did he say? Oh my God!"*

*I finally close the fridge and then rest my back against it. "He didn't kiss me."*

*"Well, what happened?"*

*"He asked how old I was."*

*"So, he's interested, because why else ask? Plus, you don't look seventeen. Look at those tits! Are you a D-cup, yet?"*

*I ignore Lee's comments. "I don't know. When I told him my age he said I wasn't old enough to drink, but I told him I was old enough for plenty more."*

*"Oh my God, you tramp!" she whisper yells.*

*"He said he was old enough to get in trouble for giving me a taste."*

*"Yeah, a taste of his cock!"*

*"That's how I took it!" I say with a laugh. "But, he gave me a sip of his beer and then walked away."*

*"What a tease."*

A car pulling up outside my gate brings me out of my reminiscing. I slide off the back of the truck, and go to the panel to open the gate.

Xavier steps out—and if possible—looks even more attractive than the last time I saw him, which was almost a year ago at my dad's funeral. But then, it was from a distance. It was like he didn't want anybody to know he was there.

"Chevelley," he states, walking towards me. "Smoking is a bad habit."

"I have lots of bad habits," I reply, blowing a smoke ring in his face.

"Do all of your bad habits have the ability to get you killed?"

"I don't know what you're talking about," I say,

throwing the cigarette to the ground and crossing my arms.

"No? What about you and your little friend pulling a gun on PJ today? You don't think that'll get you killed?"

"Hey! PJ approached us, so you blame him for that shit."

"Did Jasper not pull a gun on him?" I don't respond. "That's what I thought."

"Oh, fuck off, Xavier! You know Roman is in the wrong in this whole fucking thing. What're we supposed to do? Get up and move?"

"Roman wants to join forces."

"What?" I shriek. "Me and my crew are supposed to work for him? I don't fucking think so."

"It's the easiest way to deal with this," he responds calmly.

"Fuck no it's not."

"What is your plan exactly?"

"None of your business. You're the fucking enemy now."

"Don't do anything that's going to get you killed," he growls.

"Why do you care? We're more than capable of taking care of ourselves, anyway."

"Roman is more capable of killing you. He has cops in his pocket, C. They will turn the other way if he chooses to blow up your entire compound here."

"Are you threatening me?" I yell. "This is my house, my crew, and my territory. Roman can go fuck himself."

"Your father wouldn't want you getting yourself killed over something like this."

"My father wouldn't have put me in this position if he didn't think I could handle it. I am not letting this go to Roman's control, and I can't believe you'd want me to," I seethe.

"Don't force my hand in this, Chevelley."

"What are you going to do?"

He breathes in deeply through his nose, his nostrils flaring and his jaw tensing. "If we're forced to fight, I'll have to kill your friends in there," he says, gesturing to the house.

"And me? You gonna kill me too?" I ask. "Either we move, work for Roman, or die? That it?"

He opens his mouth to answer, but the front door slams behind us.

"What the fuck is going on out here?" Gage bellows. "What do you want, X?"

"Roman wants us to join forces, AKA, give him control. We'd be his crew," I say, anger dripping from every word. "Either we do that or die. Isn't that right, Xavier?"

"You're kidding, right?" Gage spits, looking at Xavier.

Xavier doesn't respond, he only stares down Gage with an icy look. The coldness in his glare rivals an Alaskan winter night.

"Well, you can tell Roman that I do not wish to hand him everything we've worked for, and I do not plan on moving either. We were here first, this is our only business, and he has many to fall back on." I step up to X. He towers over all of my five feet and five inches with his six feet, but I don't care. I peer up into those warm brown eyes and stick my finger into his chest. "We. Aren't. Going. Anywhere."

He glances down at my finger with a look that says he's not amused. "Then you've just started a war."

Xavier looks me up and down before turning around and walking back to his car. I run my fingers through my hair, pulling it slightly in frustration.

"Fuck! Come on," I say to Gage, moving towards the door.

When I storm into the house, Jasper, Silas, and Deacon are all gathered in the living room.

"What happened?" Jasper asks.

"You just started a fucking war with Roman, that's what happened," Gage growls, pointing a stiff finger in Jasper's direction.

"*I* started a war?" he shouts. "I didn't do shit."

I put my hand up. "Roman wants us to 'join forces,' and I said hell no. It was either that, or move away and start over somewhere else. And, I don't know about you guys, but West Philly is home, and I'm not going anywhere. X threatened that if we didn't do what Roman wanted, we'd all die."

That gets the guys all riled up. "Fuck that mother fucker. Rome's the one who's gonna die," Silas states angrily.

"I'm not moving anywhere," Deacon announces.

"Me either."

"I ain't going anywhere."

Everybody agrees they don't want to move.

"You know what that means then," I say seriously.

"I'll call the other guys," Gage announces.

"What are we gonna do first?" Deacon asks.

"I need to talk to Johnny and Lou first."

Johnny and Lou are two of the oldest people involved in this racket, both being in their late fifties. They were friends with my father when they were all in their twenties, just starting out in this underworld shit. My father hired our current group several years back, training them under the old guys until they were ready, and the other ones ready to retire.

"Rome's not gonna make a move first," Silas says. "He'll wait until we do something he doesn't approve of."

"What if we never do anything?" Jasper asks.

"Doing our job will be something he doesn't approve of," I say.

"Then what?" Jasper questions.

"With Rome, who knows? He'll kill someone. One of us. Maybe he'll fuck with one of our cars or houses, whatever he can get his hands on first. We need to be careful, and never be caught out alone. Take your gun with you everywhere you go and keep your eyes open."

"You think X will really carry out these orders?" Silas asks.

I remember the way he looked outside. The look he gave me was ominous. He's formidable, especially with Roman behind him.

"He will," I answer. "He threatened to kill all my friends if I forced his hand."

"But you and him . . ."

I shoot Silas a glare that tells him to stop talking.

"Xavier is different now. We all know that."

"The reason why he's different should be the reason why he shouldn't be . . ."

Silas is cut off when Gage comes in.

"Alright. I called Lou and Johnny, and they're on their way. Jai, Trax, and Rem are gonna be by later, so everybody needs to stay here."

We all settle in and wait for the rest of the group to arrive. Gage and Silas sit in front of the TV, and I grab a couple beers from the fridge and hand one to Deacon who's leaning against the counter. Twisting off my cap, I throw it into the sink and take a swig.

"What's goin' on, Deac?" I ask.

"Just wondering what all's gonna happen now."

He opens his bottle and takes a large gulp.

"We stay together, and we watch each other's backs, but you know what we have to do to keep Rome from killing us."

He nods. "Kill him first."

"Not just him."

He nods again. "He has a lot of loyal people around him."

"I know for the most part we've been able to do what we do without killing people. Not many, anyway. Threaten them with violence? Yes. Scare them, fight them? Definitely. But, with this . . ." I pause and take a drink, "we most definitely have to kill people."

"X included?" he asks.

I stand there staring into Deacon's green eyes unable to vocalize the answer I know I need to say.

"He's Roman's closest friend," I state.

Deacon studies me and then gives me a single nod before finishing his beer. "Okay, then."

The door opens and I hear Lou's voice thunder through the house.

"Get your asses in here and let's figure this shit out."

"Nice to see you, too, Lou," Jasper jokes.

"You. Shut up."

When we all gather around the couch, Johnny and Lou stay standing in front of us.

"Alright, we're up to speed on what's going on," Johnny announces. "Roman is prepared to kill every last one of us if that's what it takes for him to expand over here. We can't let that happen. What we're going to do is make a few calls to some of our clients. We've worked for them for all these years, and I have no doubt they'll have our backs."

The room falls quiet. Our clients are people involved in all aspects of organized crime, and not just some small street gangs and little shit. Some of our clients are big time mobsters. Scary mother fuckers.

Even though Johnny and Lou are both in their fifties, they're still intimidating men. Johnny's a little hefty in the middle, and his hair is thinning at the top, but you don't fuck with him unless you want a punch to the face. Lou on the other hand is more fit, his hair graying on the sides, and his nose is a little large for his face.

"Now, Roman has his own people, including—but not limited to—a few cops. We all know how ruthless he is, so we can't just go into this all willy-nilly. That means keep your weapons hidden unless necessary."

He pins Jasper with a chill-inducing look.

"We're pairing up," Lou announces. "If you go anywhere, you will not go alone. I don't give a fuck who you go somewhere with, but you *will* go with someone. If we can stay low and not gain any of Roman's attention, we should be fine until we talk to our clients, get a firm plan, and figure out how and when to execute it."

"And by that, you mean execute them," Silas states.

"It's them or us," Lou deadpans.

Johnny looks up at me and by the look on his face, I can tell he's going to say something I won't like.

"Chevelley, I don't know if I want you involved in this."

"What?" I bellow. "What do you mean you don't want me involved in this? This is my shit!" I exclaim.

"Memphis wouldn't want you to get hurt."

"My dad is dead now, and he was sure to let you all know that I'm in charge. Me." I point a finger at my chest. "If he didn't think I could handle anything that would come up, he wouldn't have put me in this position. I've been trained for this job my whole life, and I'll be damned if I sit back and let you all fight for me."

Johnny and Lou exchange a look while the other guys stare back at me. My body is vibrating in anger.

"C, you could get killed. Your dad would never want that, and you're like a niece to Lou and I. We can't see you die, too."

My anger recedes only slightly, because I know they consider me family, and I can understand where they're coming from, but one thing still remains. I'm in charge. I will not sit back and do nothing.

"Lou, Johnny," I say, coming closer. "I understand. I do. But, you have to understand how that makes me look as a leader. I will not sit back like a helpless, scared woman. I'm neither of those things, and not only can I protect myself, I can protect others, too."

Johnny runs a hand over his face and Lou crosses his arms over his chest and stares at me.

Gage steps up to my side "I'll stay near her anytime she's out. Nobody will dare fuck with the both of us," he says with a slight grin while elbowing me.

"You know it's not just Roman we're facing, right?" Lou asks. "Xavier is next to him at all times."

I throw my arms in the air. "God, can everybody stop bringing up Xavier! I know that he works with him. I know! Let's get this out there and never bring it up again." I make sure to look at everyone in the room. "X and I have a past. Nothing to brag about. I knew him when I was a teenager. I was young, dumb, and wanted attention. I sought it out from the wrong guy, okay? I'm over it and he's definitely over it. If anything, you should all be aware that I fucking hate Xavier now. His involvement in this doesn't make me hesitant."

Nobody says anything and I'm glad the Xavier conversation doesn't go any further, because I'm not sure they believe me anyway. I'm not sure I believe me.

"Well, I'll give you a call once I hear back from some people," Johnny says as he moves towards the front door. "You all be safe."

"Bye, Lou. Bye, Johnny," I say, and go and give them both a hug.

"You know we just care about you, right?" Johnny

says in my ear.

"Yeah. I know. I'm a big girl, though."

He gives me a small smile. "We know."

Once they leave, the guys start drinking, so I go upstairs and give Levi a call. I could use some more estrogen in this house, and since she's pretty much the only female I can stand, I invite her over.

She's gonna flip once she finds out about X. I prepare myself for another conversation regarding him, but she's the only one who truly knows what went on between Xavier and me.

"Hey, bitch!" she answers.

"Hey. Can you come over?"

"Sounds serious."

"Life or death."

"I'm coming. Be there soon."

# CHAPTER 3

"COME ON, LEE. WHEN YOU gonna give a guy a chance?"

I hear Deacon's voice float up the stairs as Lee opens my door.

"When you can stop fucking skank bitches, and since I just saw you with one yesterday, looks like never."

Lee comes in and gives me a smile, slamming my door behind her.

"Deac coming on to you again?" I ask as I scoot up on my bed and lean against the headboard.

She rolls her eyes. "He's crazy."

"You like him, though," I say with a smirk.

"Anyway," she says, changing the subject. "What's going on with you?"

She sits on the bed by my feet and looks at me over the tops of my knees.

I sigh and then look up at the ceiling, trying to figure out what to say first. Levi's been around forever, so she knows the shit we're all involved in, and while she isn't involved, she doesn't judge the way we make a living.

"Looks like we got a war going with Roman and his crew."

She pulls my knees apart and looks at me with wide eyes. "What?"

I drop my legs flat on the bed on each side of her. "Roman wanted us to join forces with him, but I can't do that. So, the only alternative is to fight and see who comes out on top."

"I don't like the sound of this, C."

"Me either."

"Well, what's the plan?"

"We're talking to some people to have our back. Our plan is to attack before being attacked."

I look up into her green eyes. Eyes that are filled with fear.

"You guys are my second family. I can't lose you."

"We're not going anywhere, Lee."

She studies my face. "What are you not telling me?"

"Xavier." I don't need to say anything else.

"Oh my gosh! I forgot. He works for Roman now." I only nod my head. "What . . . I mean, how, what the fuck?" she finally says.

"He was over here earlier."

"Did you kick him in the fucking balls?"

I smile. "No, but I should have."

"Fuckin' right, you should have."

"He's so different."

"Can you blame him, though?" she asks.

"He threatened my friends, Lee. He said he'd kill them all if I forced his hand."

She looks surprised for a second. "I don't even know what to say, C."

"Fuck it. Let's go get fucked up and just forget about it before we can't ignore it any longer."

"Sounds like a plan."

We both jog down the stairs and the guys in the living room all turn and look at us.

"You two are a sight for sore eyes," Jai says, bringing his beer to his mouth.

"Stop looking at C like that," Gage threatens.

I roll my eyes. "I'm still a woman, Gage."

"No, you're not."

All the guys laugh, used to Gage's overprotective ways.

"You can look at me however you want, Jai," Lee says, going over and giving him a hug.

I see Deacon's jaw clench and I can't help but laugh. I know Lee's doing that on purpose. Jai is a cool guy, but he has a girlfriend. He's just flirtatious with everybody.

Lee stays pressed to his side, her arm wrapped around his waist, and takes a swig of his beer. Jai's milk chocolate skin is free of ink; the only one of us with no tattoos. Lee's milky white skin is on display with her short denim shorts and tank top. Her blonde hair falls over her shoulders, and she winks at Deacon across the room.

I grab her arm and pull her into the kitchen.

"You trying to piss Deac off?" I ask as I pull some liquor from the oak cabinet.

She shrugs. "He pisses me off all the time."

"You guys are ridiculous. What do you want to drink?"

"You have any of that Red Berry Ciroc?"

"Yep."

I pull the large bottle out and grab some Cran-Grape juice and mix us both a drink.

"Shot first?" she asks with a grin.

I smile and pour two shots of Ciroc.

With liquor already running through our systems, and a full drink in our hands, we make our way back into the living room with the guys.

"Move it," I say as I nudge Silas.

"Bossy ass," he mumbles before scooting over on the couch.

"Thanks," I chirp, giving him a big smile.

"Where am I supposed to sit?" Lee asks.

"Deacon's lap," I say, pointing at Deacon sitting in the chair behind her.

She glares at me.

"Come on, Lee. You know you want to," Deac says, resting both arms on the arms of the chair and waiting for Lee's move.

Lee walks over to him, but instead of sitting on his lap, she pushes his arm and sits on the arm of the chair. Deacon laughs, but doesn't say anything else.

"You okay?" Silas asks me quietly.

"Just not thinking about it right now."

"Alright."

I look around the room and watch my friends let loose one last time. This will be the last time we're all going to be able to drink, relax, and have fun for who knows how long. I know the shit with Roman is in the back of everybody's head, but we deserve one more night to just have fun and spend time together. This is our family. Some of us don't have anybody else, and Johnny and Lou are at home with their own families. Jai's on the phone arguing with his girlfriend like usual. She doesn't like hanging out with us, so they're always off and on. Gage is standing behind the couch talking to Trax about some new truck he wants, and Trax is pretending to be interested.

Trax is thirty years old and only into muscle cars. His black hair is just now growing back from buzzing it down to his scalp, and his light green eyes light his whole face up. He's pale, but it makes his colorful tattoos stand out even more. He's the perfect canvas for a tattoo artist. He glances over Gage's shoulder and gives me a wink. Gage continues talking about this truck and I point my fingers at my temple like I'm going to shoot myself and right as I make a face, Gage turns around and catches me.

"Fuck off, C," he laughs.

The door opens, gaining all of our attention and Rem walks in holding a case of beer and a bottle of Captain Morgan.

"Hey, fuckers!" he announces.

Rem—short for Remington—is twenty-eight years old and has the body of a god. He's got long, blonde hair, and beautiful blue eyes. He has one of the best personalities of the group. Easy to get along with, funny, and laid back.

"Hey, Rem! What you got for me?" I ask.

"Whatever you want, darlin'" he says with a smirk.

I roll my eyes. "I think I want the Captain more."

"Damn, that's rough, Rem," Jai laughs.

"She knows she wants my captain more," Rem replies, thrusting his hips forward.

"I'd prefer four star general. Now give me my Morgan."

"I can give you an eight inch general," he continues.

"Knock it off, Rem!" Gage scolds.

I give Rem a smirk and he hands over the liquor. "Where you been anyway?" I ask him.

"I had to grab more drinks for you lazy asses."

"Probably get some ass, too," Lee says.

"Jealous?" Rem asks.

"Hardly. I don't tend to get jealous of STD infected vaginas."

"Whatever, Lee. You're just mad you ain't getting any."

Rem walks to the kitchen to put the beer away, but when he comes back he pulls me up, drops to my seat, and then pulls me across his lap. Typical Rem behavior.

"You know you shouldn't have been out there alone,"

I tell him.

"I wasn't alone," he says with a grin. "I have my good friend Beretta with me, and my other good friend, Ruger."

I push his head. "That's the last time you're going out alone."

"You comin' with me next time?" he asks, once again thrusting his hips, causing me to bounce up on his lap.

"Are you always horny?" I ask with a shake of my head.

"I'm a guy," he says, lifting one shoulder up.

"Whatever," I say with a laugh as I push up off of him.

Rem has always flirted with me, but really he flirts with everybody. Okay, he probably flirts with me more because we have hooked up in the past. Gage doesn't know. In fact, nobody knows.

What I like about Rem is he isn't intimidated by me. He isn't intimidated by anyone. He gets my personality, he understands the job I do, and we've been friends a while. There aren't any feelings between us, and we both know it isn't going to be anything serious.

"Want to play a game?" Lee asks.

"What kind of game?"

"Shot roulette."

"What the fuck is shot roulette?" Silas asks.

"We fill up some shot glasses with different kinds of liquor, you can even put beer in some, or water or juice. You put them in a large circle and spin a bottle in the middle and whatever it lands on you have to drink."

Her face lights up with a huge smile, showing her excitement. The guys look at each other like it's a terrible idea.

"Let's do it!" I say, already walking to the kitchen.

Lee and I get all the shot glasses filled and take them

to the large table in the dining area.

"Guys! Come on!" Lee shouts.

The guys come in, a mixture of grumbling about the game, and laughing because some are already drunk.

"Who goes first?" Deacon asks.

"Me, of course," she says, turning to the bottle and giving it a good spin.

It lands on something dark and she carefully picks it up and smells it before downing it.

"What was it?" I ask, my face scrunching up because of the look on her face.

"Hennessey, I think. God. Ah!" she coughs.

All the guys laugh and then Deacon leans in and spins the bottle. "Stop being a baby," he jokes, waiting for the bottle to stop.

He picks up the shot glass and drinks it down without smelling it. His face is probably more priceless than Lee's was.

Lee puts her hands on her hips and smirks at him. "Good?" she asks.

"What the fuck did you guys put in here?" he asks, making a sour face.

"You must have had the lemon juice," I say with a laugh.

"This game is dumb," he says, drinking his beer.

I go next and end up getting my Morgan. Gage goes after me and gets watermelon vodka, which he hates. We're each able to go two times, most of us getting at least one liquor and one non-liquor drink. I think Deacon got both non-liquor, so he's not a fan of the game. Since everybody was already drinking before playing the game, we're all feeling pretty buzzed and happy.

We move back to the living room, blast some music, and enjoy our night together. Lee's flirting with Deacon more, probably because of the alcohol, but everybody knows she likes him. A few of the guys go into our bonus room and start playing pool on a table we have in there. Rem and I are sitting on the couch together, sharing a mixed drink.

"Wanna fuck?" He asks so casually, it makes me bark out a laugh.

"Uh. No."

"Too much for you?" he asks through his own laughter.

"Shut up, Rem," I say as I nudge him in the side.

"Is this shit weighing on you? For real, you can tell me the truth," he says, his voice becoming serious.

"Yeah. I don't like what it's coming to. I'm worried."

"What all are you worried about?"

"Losing some of you."

"You're not gonna lose me. Nobody can take me down," he says in his typical cocky tone.

"This is Roman and Xavier," I say on a sigh.

"So what? I'll kill both of those fuckers at the same time. I'm not going to let anything happen to you or our crew. You should know that we all have your back, C."

"I know," I say with a small smile and rest my head on his shoulder.

He rubs my thigh, tracing the sugar skull tattoo that covers most of it.

"Yo, Rem! Come get your ass kicked in pool real quick," Gage's voice shouts from the other room.

"You okay?" he asks as he stands up.

"Yep. Go get your ass kicked."

He taps my knee and then turns to walk away.

"I'm not sure why you think you're king shit at pool anyway, Gage. I beat you last time."

"Only because I scratched on the eight ball. You had four fucking balls still on the table."

"A win is a win," Rem says before he enters the other

room.

I take another swig of my drink and notice that I'm the only one in the living room. I stand up to go find Lee and find I'm a little unsteady on my feet. I probably should've had more to eat before I started drinking. I place the glass on the table and make my way to the fridge to get some water. My phone vibrates in the back pocket of my shorts, and once I down almost the whole bottle of water, I pull it out and check it.

It's from an unknown number which automatically makes me uncomfortable. I swipe my phone to unlock it and view the text.

> *Don't say anything to anybody, just leave the house and walk out the front gate. Now.*

My heart hammers in my chest. Roman? Maybe Xavier? But why? It's obvious there are a lot of people here, so why come now? Then again, whoever it is was clear to make sure I go out alone without telling anyone. Do they just want to kill me? I can go and protect everyone else, or tell them and possibly get a lot of people hurt.

Whether it's a stupid decision or not, I go upstairs and grab my gun, tucking it in the back of my shorts, making sure my long and loose black tank covers it up. I'm able to get through the house without anyone noticing me.

The darkness surrounds me as soon as I step out. The night sky is an inky black with almost no stars in sight. It's cloudy, like a storm is brewing somewhere nearby. How ironic.

I slowly make my way to the front gate and look out before opening it, but I don't see any cars. Boots on gravel startle me and I snap my head to the right and see a man in all black walking towards me.

"Open the gate and come out."

# CHAPTER 4

XAVIER.

I take a deep breath and unlock the gate before sliding through a small opening.

"What are you doing here?" I ask.

Xavier doesn't speak right away. He pulls a pack of cigarettes from his pocket and I watch quietly as he goes through the motions. When he puts it in his mouth, his hand comes up to light it and the small flame allows me to see that his eyes are pinned to mine. After taking a deep inhale and blowing the smoke into the air, he finally speaks.

"Have you reconsidered our offer?"

I'm shocked speechless for a few moments. "Are you serious?"

He nods once, taking another drag.

"No. Your offer is still as shitty as it was earlier."

"I'm trying to help you, Chevelley." His voice is low and rough.

"Really? That's what help looks like nowadays? Threats of murder? Huh. No, thank you."

A growl emits from his throat. "You're lucky I'm even here making sure you want to go through with this. I don't do this kind of shit. If you get your people to go against Roman, there's going to be a lot of dead bodies in your wake. You think you can handle that?"

I focus on the first part of his statement. "So, if you don't do this, then why are you here?"

He sucks in another hit of the tobacco, his eyes never leaving my face. His jaw is tense, his eyes are penetrating as he looks at me. He's everything you should be afraid of, everything you should stay away from, and you can tell just by looking at him that he's dangerous. It's the exact reason I was drawn to him in the first place.

"You shouldn't question my kindness."

"Why?" I ask, risking the chance of pissing him off.

He takes another drag and walks right up to me. Stubble covers his jaw and he smells of nicotine and mint. His honey-colored eyes rake over my body, and a familiar feeling forms in my stomach and another place a little south of there.

His arm snakes around my waist so fast, and before I know it, he has my own gun pointed at my head.

"Because I can kill you before you even realize it's happening," he says, answering the question I regret asking.

I step back and he lets the gun dangle from his finger as he holds it out for me. The cigarette in his mouth hangs on his lip, the smoke filtering up into his face.

Snatching the gun from him, I straighten my posture and keep the gun in hand.

"Thanks for extending me your kindness then," I snarl. "But, the next time I see you, I could very well be the one who takes *you* out before you realize it's happening."

A slow, menacing smile forms on his face. "Sure." He turns on his heel and starts to disappear into the darkness. Right before he's no longer visible, he turns around and says, "Stay as far away from me as possible. I mean it. You're going to get yourself killed."

I'm about to rattle on about why he should care or how he's the one who showed up to my place, but he's gone before I can open my mouth. I hear his motorcycle start up and realize he must have parked around the corner.

Before people start to notice my absence, I make my way back into the house, but I'm no longer in the mood to party. I jog upstairs, but before I can open my door, I hear Rem call my name.

"What?" I ask, looking to the bottom of the stairs.

"Wanna fuck?" he asks with a charming smile.

Don't ask how he can ask a woman to have sex in that way and still look charming, but Rem pulls it off.

"Come on," I answer without a second thought.

Why the fuck not?

I quickly toss my gun on my dresser and kick my shoes off. As soon as Rem walks in, he kicks the door closed behind him and pulls his T-shirt off in one quick movement. The bright tattoos across his chest are eye-catching. His muscles ripple with each movement, and he rips my shirt off in the same manner.

"Fuck, C. These tits get my dick so hard," he says, squeezing my breasts in his large hands.

Rem quickly unhooks my bra allowing it to fall to the floor, and I pull off my shorts while he takes his pants and boxers off.

Once he gets the condom on, he backs me up against the door.

"Fuck me, Rem," I pant, needing to get lost in rough sex.

"You got it, babe," he answers before quickly thrusting his long cock into me.

My legs wrap around his waist while he has both hands under my ass, holding me up. Rem fucks me hard and rough. I pull on his long hair, gaining hisses and grunts from his mouth. He pulls me from the door and takes the few steps to my bed and half drops me before positioning himself between my legs.

His hand squeezes my large breasts and he sucks my pierced nipple into his mouth before tugging on the silver bar with his teeth.

Rem sits back on his knees and pushes both of my legs up near my head and pushes his thick length into me in hard thrusts.

"Fuck, C," he grunts. "I could fuck your pussy all night."

I moan and dig my nails into his thighs. He props one leg on his shoulder, letting the other fall to the bed, and his free hand comes up and rubs circles on my clit.

My orgasm builds as his thrusts become harder and deeper. "Yes, yes," I chant. "God, yes."

A few seconds later, I'm crying out and clenching around him. He growls and grunts, fucking me faster, and a couple minutes after I've come down from my orgasm, he tenses and releases himself inside of my throbbing pussy.

After he gets up to get his clothes on, I find a clean shirt and underwear and slip them on. He drops onto the edge of my bed and gives me a smirk.

"I knew you wanted to fuck."

"Shut up," I say with a laugh.

"You goin' to sleep?" he asks.

"Yeah."

"Okay, well, I'll see you tomorrow."

"Alright."

He leans forward and kisses my forehead before leaving the room.

I love the relationship Rem and I have. We care about each other as friends, and fuck on occasion, but don't have any pre-conceived ideas about what we are to each other. We are what we are. We don't hook up regularly, but I'm glad neither of us feels used or awkward afterwards.

As I fall asleep, I don't think about the blonde-haired, blue-eyed god that fucks like I imagine a god would, but instead the man in black fills my mind.

Xavier.

Always in black.

Inky hair.

Dark eyes.

Black soul.

WHEN I GET DOWNSTAIRS THE next morning, a couple bodies are lain across the couches. Beer bottles and cans are littered throughout the house, and it reeks of smoke and spilled liquor. This is the bad thing about living with men, they don't fucking clean a goddamn thing. I don't even want to look at the bathrooms right now.

I kick the couch Jai is sleeping on. "You gonna help me clean?"

He groans, turning onto his side. "Now?"

"Yes, now. Why are you even here?" I ask, making my way to the kitchen.

"My lady got mad at me."

"Huh. Not surprised." I come back in and drop a black trash bag on him. "Start throwing shit in there."

He mumbles something and slowly gets to his feet. After he's cleared the tables of bottles and cans, I wipe them down and dump ashtrays into the trash. I clean the kitchen and vacuum the floors while he takes all the trash out.

Deacon stumbles in the room, squinting his eyes like

he's just walked into the sun.

"Really, C? The vacuum at this time?"

I shut it off and put my hand on my hip. "It's noon, Deac, and unless you're going to clean this house, then yes, the vacuum at this time."

He raises his hands in defeat. "Okay."

"You can clean the bathroom down here. I'm sure you guys fucked it all up."

"Ugh. I hate coming over here. You always try to put us all to work."

"I try to make you be responsible."

"Whatever. I'll do it in a little bit."

"Thanks. So, you and Lee?"

He looks up and the side of his mouth curves. "I'm working on it. She's gonna submit to me soon. I can feel it."

I roll my eyes. "Good luck with that."

"Gage and Silas around?" he asks.

I shrug. "In their rooms, I guess."

Moving towards the couch, I collapse into the large cushions and Deacon does the same.

"How do you feel about this whole getting mobsters involved thing?" he asks.

It takes me a few seconds to respond. "It makes me nervous. I know Lou and Johnny will only contact people they trust, but can you really trust mobsters? I'm afraid they might be on Roman's side and double-cross us. Then again, if they can truly help, we could use it."

Deacon sighs. "Yeah."

We don't say anything else. There's not much else to be said. We understand the situation and how fucked up it is. A few minutes later, Silas and Gage come downstairs, both looking showered and dressed.

"Chelle, you know I would've helped with the cleaning," Gage says, looking around the living room.

"It's cool. I got Jai to help, and Deac is gonna clean the bathroom," I say, nudging Deacon in the side.

"Yeah, and I'm really excited about it," he mumbles.

"Well, I just got off the phone with Lou. He's already started talking to some people."

"Yeah? And how's that going?" I ask.

"Good. Everybody he's talked to so far is on board to help us. They have their own issues with Roman, so we shouldn't have to worry about anyone switching sides."

"Who?" Deacon asks.

"The Carters up in Chicago, the Muccino brothers in New York, and Mario Ambrossi who lives here in Philly."

"Not bad," I say.

"Nah, not bad at all," Silas chimes in. "We're going to figure out when we can get them here, but first we need to track Roman's movements. We need to know where and when we can get him and most of his crew at the same time."

"Trax," Deac and I say at the same time.

Trax got his name from being so good at tracking people down. His real name is Trey, but nobody ever calls him that.

"But we need someone to be with Trax, just in case."

"I'll go," Deac replies. "I'm better than Jasper, and you two are too noticeable," he says, gesturing at the two giant men.

"Alright, then. You guys need to go out there today and start watching him. We don't know when he's going to start making moves, so we need to be vigilant. Check in with us on the hour. I'll call Trax now."

Gage walks to the kitchen, already dialing Trax's number, and Deacon gets up to use the bathroom, and in his own words, "try to wipe up some of the piss."

"Rem left by himself last night," Silas says as he sits

next to me. "We didn't realize it till later."

I sigh heavily. "He never wants to listen."

"He thinks he's Rambo or some shit."

"Is he okay?"

"He's fine. I already talked to him. He said he didn't want to sleep on the floor all night, so he just went home."

"What about Lee?" I ask, feeling bad that I didn't even tell her I was going to sleep last night.

"We got her a cab, and Trax went with her. She called me when she got there to let us know she was safe, and then Trax went home from there."

"Okay, good."

"Where's Jai?" Silas asks.

"Okay, Trax is on his way over now." Gage says, walking up behind us. "He and Deac should start off near The Shed. I know for a fact that he does a lot of his business out of there. He's bound to leave or show up at some point."

"Yeah, and if he's not at the bar, he spends some time over at Wild Mary's," Silas states.

"Ew. Wild Mary's? That's the nastiest strip joint here. I'm afraid I'll catch herpes from just walking in there." I say with a scrunched up face.

The men just shrug. I guess a naked woman is a naked woman, no matter where her nasty snatch has been.

"Silas and I are going to go meet with Lou and Johnny. You need to come, Chelle. Trax and Deac are about to leave, and I'll make sure Jasper stays here. Lord knows we don't need him of all people being seen."

"Yeah, let me just get dressed," I say, pushing up from the couch.

"Rem's at home and where's Jai?" Gage asks.

"He went to take out the trash," I say slowly, realizing he went out there a while back. "He should have been back inside by now."

We all take a quick glance at each other.

"The dumpster is just at the corner," Gage states.

Each of us moves quickly to the door. Gage and Silas have their guns, but I'm not sure about Deacon. I know mine is upstairs, but I grab a tire iron from the back of Gage's truck.

We rush through the open gate, and make our way to where the dumpster is.

The trash is on the ground.

Blood is on the ground.

We look around, but there's nothing or nobody else to be seen.

"Fuck!"

# CHAPTER 5

THE BLOOD BOILS BENEATH MY skin. My flesh feels hot and my heart thunders rapidly in my chest.

"Son of a bitch!" I yell, running to my room to change and grab my gun.

I bang on Jasper's door before swinging it open. It crashes against the wall, startling him awake.

"What the fuck?" he asks drowsily.

"Get the fuck up and downstairs. Now."

I jog down the stairs where Gage, Silas, and Deacon are all coming up with a plan.

"Okay, it wasn't a lot of blood. He could still be alive. We need to get people over at Wild Mary's and The Shed. And, even though this is quite dangerous, we need to have people near his house."

"Okay, I'll take Jasper," I say. "You and Silas go to The Shed, and Trax and Deac can go to Wild Mary's. Between all of us, we should see movement soon. Keep your cells on you, but on vibrate. We need to stay in constant communication. The minute we don't hear from someone, we need to go to that location and make sure nothing has happened. Got it?"

Everybody nods and Jasper comes down the stairs.

"What's going on?"

"You're coming with me. Got your gun?"

"Yeah."

We all rush out and get into our cars and head to our respective locations. I'm too angry to speak, so I don't tell Jasper anything right away. He has the good sense to not ask me either. It isn't until I'm closer to Roman's that I say anything.

"Roman has Jai. We don't know details, but he never came back from taking the trash out, and there was blood. We're watching the places we know Roman's known to be."

Roman's place is huge and secured well. I pull up on a street across and a little diagonally from it. I have the perfect view of the front of his home without being directly in front of it. The windows on the Impala are tinted as dark as they can be, so nobody can see in. I text Gage and Deacon to let them know I'm in place and get similar responses.

Now, we wait.

"C, I'm sorry," Jasper says.

I raise my hand to stop him. "Don't. It doesn't matter anymore, okay? This war with Roman would have happened anyway."

I rub my sweaty palms over my dark, denim jeans. My hands are shaking out of anger and out of nerves. If anything happens to Jai, or has happened to him already, I won't be able to feel anything but guilt. I made him help me and had him take out the trash. I had no idea somebody would be waiting at the corner. I thought it was safe enough to at least take out some trash. I was wrong. Boy, how I was wrong.

My phone vibrates in the console.

"Gage? What's up?"

"One of Rome's cars just showed up, someone went in for a few minutes, and it's leaving now. We're following it, but it looks like it might be going to his house.

Keep an eye out."

"Okay. Be careful."

"Somebody might be heading this way," I tell Jasper when I hang up.

"Rome?"

"Don't know. It's one of his cars, though."

Five minutes later, I get a text saying Gage and Silas lost the vehicle due to an accident, and that they'll be on their way as soon as they can.

Another ten minutes goes by and then we see a black Lincoln pull into the driveway of Roman's house. Jasper leans forward, trying to get a good look at whoever comes out of that car.

The passenger side isn't visible. They've pulled up to where that side of the car is facing the door, so unless anybody comes out of the driver's side, we won't see anyone.

I tap my fingers on the steering wheel impatiently. Suddenly, the driver's door opens, and while I normally wouldn't care who the driver is, this time it's different.

Xavier steps out of the car, looks around, and then closes the door and walks around to the back. We lose track of him briefly, but then he's back, climbing into the driver's seat.

"Is that . . ." Jasper starts.

"Yep."

We watch as he drives the car into the grass along the side of the house and disappears behind the massive structure.

"What's back there?" Jasper asks.

"Don't know, but we need to find out."

I text Gage and tell him my plan and then slide the phone in my back pocket as I hop out of the car.

"What are you doing?" Jasper asks in a harsh whisper.

"We have to see where he went and what he's doing. I can't drive over there, so I'm going to try to go around the back."

Jasper runs a hand over his face and then follows behind me. I jog to the end of the street away from Rome's place. I make my way to the narrow alleyway behind the houses on his street. We both pause to take in the area, guns in hand, and then move quietly towards his house.

When we get closer to what's Roman's backyard, I'm disappointed to see there's a large, concrete fence that keeps everything completely hidden. It's got to be about eight or nine feet high.

"Get on my shoulders," Jasper whispers.

I tuck my gun in the back of my pants and Jasper bends down to allow me to climb onto his shoulders. With his height just over six feet, I might be able to see something. He steps right up to the fence but I can barely see anything. I have to put my hands on the top of the thick concrete and pull myself up.

Doing so slowly, my head peeks over the top and I see the black Lincoln parked in front of a semi large shed that sits in the corner of the backyard. My eyes scan the rest of the area and I don't see anybody around. There's some French doors at the back of the house, but it looks like the blinds are closed.

"See anything?" Jasper whispers.

"Not really," I reply quietly. "Move over a few steps so I can see around this tree."

Jasper moves to the right, and I'm sure to hang onto the fence so I don't topple over. There's a large tree in the yard that blocks a good portion of the area. As soon as he takes his third step to the right, my heart stops.

"Shit!" I whisper yell and duck my head. "There's people there."

I feel Jasper bend down, but I stay on his shoulders. I hear voices, but can't make out what they're saying. There was only two people and I didn't look long enough to see who it was. Even though my heart is beating hard in my chest, I want to stick around a bit longer to find out if they have Jai or not.

A minute later, a door closes loudly, so I straighten up and try peering over the fence again. For a few seconds I don't see anything, but then I see Xavier come out of the house holding a tool of some sort and walk to the shed.

"I think Jai might be in the shed," I tell Jasper. "Xavier just went in there."

"What do you want to do?"

Before I can respond, I hear a loud crash in the shed that makes me jump. I'm stunned silent for a few seconds. When I find my voice, I say the only thing that comes to mind. "We have to get in there."

"Maybe we should wait for Gage and . . ." Jasper starts.

The shed door opens and I shush him. I watch with wide eyes as Xavier exits with the same tool in his hand, except now it's got blood on it.

"Mother fucker."

Xavier's head turns and he looks back in my direction. I instantly duck my head behind the concrete.

"Let me down. We gotta go!" I whisper sternly.

Jasper quickly drops lower and helps me off his shoulders.

"What happened?" he demands as we start to jog down the alleyway.

"I'm not sure if he saw me or not."

We hear a lock clinking on a gate and I know we won't make it to the end of the block without being seen.

"Hide behind the dumpster," Jasper says.

We sprint to the dumpster on the other side of the

alley and squat on the side. Pulling our guns out, we wait to see if he follows us. My breathing is heavy, but I try to stay as quiet as possible.

I hear slow footsteps crunching over the gravel. Xavier will see us in no more than ten seconds if he continues walking. If that happens, I just have to be the one to shoot first.

The unmistakable sound of a gun cocking seems to echo through the small area. His footsteps have stopped along with my breathing. My grip on the gun tightens, and I try not to shift my feet and make any noise.

One more step sends rocks flying, one of them hitting the dumpster we're crouching behind. I close my eyes briefly and take a deep breath.

I can step out from behind the dumpster and try to save Jasper's life by pretending I'm alone, or I can sit here and wait and see if Xavier kills us both on sight. I'd like to think Xavier wouldn't shoot me, but at this point, I'm not so sure. He's proven he's not opposed to kidnapping and hurting my friends.

Making the decision to save Jasper if I can, I move to stand up and catch the scent of Xavier floating through the air. He's close. Really close.

"X! What're you doing?" A voice yells from Roman's house.

I stay in place and see the side of his shoe as he turns to yell back. "Nothing. I'm coming."

He pauses for a few seconds before turning back. I hear his steps get further and further away, and as soon as I hear the gate close, I let out a sigh of relief.

"Fuck," Jasper breathes as he lets his body collapse against the dumpster.

"Yeah, we need to get out of here, but I'm afraid he might go look out front and he'll see us run to the car. I'm gonna text Gage and see if he can pick us up somewhere nearby."

"Well, let's at least get out of this alley," he says.

I peek around the dumpster just to make sure Xavier is really gone, and then our feet are hitting the gravel, taking us to the end of the alley. We go in the opposite direction of where our car is parked, and farther away from Roman's house.

Gage responds that he's close, so Jasper and I wait two roads over until he shows up.

"What happened?" Gage demands as soon as we slide into the backseat.

"I'm pretty sure they're holding Jai in a shed behind the house. I saw Xavier drive the car back there, and then when we came to check it out, I saw him walk into the shed with a tool. Some sort of mallet. After a loud crash and a couple minutes, he came out and it was obvious there was blood on it."

"So, what's the plan?" Jasper asks.

After a few seconds, I respond. "We come back at night and get into the shed. We need to get Jai out of there."

"Well, let's get some guys together and get a plan. We can't think we can just jump the fence, grab him, and escape without any problems," Gage says.

I nod once and then I'm left with my guilty thoughts.

It's my fault Jai is where he is, and it's my job to get him out. Even if I have to sacrifice myself.

# CHAPTER 6

"HEY, IT'S NOT YOUR FAULT," Rem tells me.

I'm pacing back and forth, biting on my thumb nail as Gage tells the rest of the guys the plan for tonight.

"It *is* my fault."

"You couldn't have known this would happen. It was right down the street for God's sake! We all would have went alone."

"I *did* know this could happen. We all did. It was careless and stupid, and I should've went with him."

Rem sighs heavily. "We're gonna get him back."

I don't try to agree, because what I'm truly afraid of is that we're going to get there and Jai will be missing, or if he's still in the shed, he'll be dead.

"I didn't think it would start so soon. I was stupid enough to think we'd have time to get our shit together before Rome did anything," I growl.

"Yeah, well, he didn't waste any time," Rem responds, running a hand through his hair in a frustrated manner. "Lou and Johnny are gonna head out of town, but when they come back, they'll be back with a couple guys who will be helping us out."

I nod. There's nothing else to say at this point.

"Hey, C. I think we're all set to go," Gage says as he walks up to us.

"Yeah? When do we leave?"

"We should leave now, get everybody where they need to be."

"Okay."

I grab my black, leather jacket and pull it on before I meet up with everyone outside. We all get into our respective cars, and with directions on what to do and where to go, we start our journey in getting Jai back.

Jasper and I ride in silence on the way to Rome's house. The seriousness of what could happen tonight weighs heavily on each of us.

The plan for tonight is for all but one of us to park our cars on different roads around Roman's house. Each of them at least a street away, but in every direction, in case we need to run to one of them. We have one guy, Deacon, who's to stay in a car outside and alert us of anything he sees happening.

We'll all sneak towards the house from every direction, and end up where we've decided on. Me and Jasper will be at the back again, while Gage and Silas are going to take the risky job of coming up from the front, and trying to go down the side of the house where X drove Jai to the shed. Roman doesn't have a gate, but he has guards, so hopefully they'll get past them without any problems.

Trax and Rem will have to split up and linger in the shadows, ready to cause a distraction if need be. If Gage and Silas can get to the backyard, then hopefully they can unlock the gate for us, but if not, Jasper will have to try to get me over the fence, and I'll have to try to jump down without making noise or hurting myself in the process.

The only thing I'm afraid of is them having dogs. We didn't see any when we were here before, but they could have been inside. Hopefully we don't run into that problem, because that will ruin everything.

Before we start our walk up the alleyway, I shoot a text to everybody, making sure we're all ready to go. When I get responses from everyone, Jasper and I head to the huge, concrete fence that holds our friend captive.

When we get there we repeat what we did earlier, and I get on his shoulders trying to see into the yard. It's fairly dark, but the faint glow of lights from the house windows shine some light across the yard. I try to crane my neck and look in the direction Gage and Silas would be coming from. We wait for what seems like forever, and with each passing second, I'm worried about what's going on with Gage and Silas.

"You're gonna have to heave me up, so I can try to climb over. I don't know when Gage and Silas will be able to get back here, but I don't want to waste any time," I whisper to Jasper.

"Just be sure to open the gate as soon as you land, so I can be in there with you."

I say I will, but in all actuality, I don't know where the gate even is. It's definitely not visible from the back.

Grasping onto the top of the fence, I get as much of my upper body up as possible and then put my feet on Jasper's shoulders until I can throw one over the top of the fence. As soon as I'm straddling the concrete, I hear a noise from the house. Throwing my body across the top, I hold on for dear life. Hopefully, with me being pressed closely to the fence they won't see any silhouette.

I soon see a man walk out onto the porch and light up a cigarette. I'm instantly hoping Gage and Silas don't make their way back here now. At least not while this man is out here.

The shadowy figure doesn't walk around or even take a seat on one of the chairs that's nearby. He just stands there, smoking his cigarette and looking around the yard. And then his eyes are on me.

In my direction at least. I can see him, and his head is clearly facing me. I feel like we're in a staring contest, only I'm hoping he's unaware of this little game. I'm hoping he can't see me out here.

A small light comes on, and I realize it's his phone. He puts it to his ear and a few seconds later he speaks.

"Yeah. I'm positive. Okay."

That's it. Those four words could mean almost anything, but for some reason I think it has to do with me. Perhaps all of us out here, because the man speaking those words is Xavier. There's no mistaking his voice. Maybe he can see me.

He finishes his cigarette and looks to the ground as he steps on it. Before he goes inside, he looks in my direction again, then he disappears into the house.

Thinking I don't have much time on my side, I jump inside the yard, and walk alongside the fence, looking for a gate. I use my hands to feel for a lock or a break in the concrete. It isn't until I'm at the corner, that I feel a space. With my eyes being as adjusted to the darkness as possible, I step back and try to examine the area.

The reason we didn't see the gate is because it's disguised as part of the fence. It looks exactly the same, except on this side there's a lock. After a few seconds of trying to get it open, I find a bolt of some sort. They've got it to where you need a key to unlock it, and that means there's nothing I can do to open it. I'm too afraid to try to speak to Jasper to let him know, so I have to leave him waiting for me.

I'm now about seven or eight feet from the shed that holds Jai. Walking slowly and carefully, I head towards the back of the small prison, and hope Gage and Silas show up soon. When I reach the back wall, I peek around to the right, trying to get a view to the front of the house.

I see the same black Lincoln parked in a way that makes it seem like they are blocking the passageway. There's definitely room to squeeze by, though, so that shouldn't hinder Gage and Silas from getting back here.

I walk around the right side of the shed, since it's hidden from view from the house, and slowly poke my head around to get a look at the door. There's two handles with a padlock connecting them.

A small noise ahead of me catches my attention. My head snaps up, and my eyes scan the area. Two large figures are gradually making their way in my direction.

Gage and Silas.

I breathe a sigh of relief at the sight of them, but it's quickly replaced with fear as the door of the house opens.

With the shed as a shield, I hold my hands up, hoping they see me, but they keep moving. I try to take a step closer to them without passing the shed. I wave my hands slightly, trying to get their attention. It seems to work, because they both stop in their tracks and push their bodies up to the side of the house.

I slink back towards the rear of the shed with my heart in my throat.

"Let's get this shit over with," a man's voice says.

The talking ceases, but I hear a soft crunch as their footsteps hit the grass. The lock on the door jingles, and I know that it's only gonna be a few seconds before they're inside and finishing Jai off. I can't stand here and let them kill Jai while I just listen and do nothing. It's my fault he's in there, so it's up to me to spare his life.

I plan on waiting for them both to go inside, and then walk up behind them and shoot them both from behind before they even know I'm there. Silas and Gage will see what I'm doing, and will be behind me in no time.

Pulling the gun from the back of my pants, I wait for

them to make noise with the door before I cock it. The opportunity comes when they pull the lock from the handles, and pull open the creaky doors.

As I cautiously make my way to the front of the shed again, I look in Silas and Gage's direction, so they know what I'm about to do.

They aren't there.

My heart beats a mile a minute. Where did they go? I panic knowing that with them not there, they won't be able to have my back, but it's a decision already made. I have to go through with it.

With one eye on the house, I step around the shed and take two steps to get to the door. Gun raised, I walk in and notice only one man is inside. His wide back is to me as he leans over a small table with a lantern on it. His body shifts slightly, and I notice Jai is sitting in a chair, his top half lying across the table.

Unsure of where the other man went, I'm grateful for the silencer, because I can take this guy out without anybody hearing, and hopefully get Jai out before the other man returns. As I begin squeezing the trigger, I hear a gun cock behind me.

"Drop it, Chevelley." Xavier's smooth voice is like a whisper.

The man in front of me whirls around while bringing his own gun out as I jump to the side.

"What the fuck?" he spits.

I stand there, my gun still trained on the man in front of me. Xavier slowly walks to the side of me, his gun pointed at my head.

"I said, drop it."

It doesn't take long, but in that moment, it feels like time stands still.

Someone walks into the shed behind me, and both Xavier and his friend tighten their aim in my direction.

At this point, it's kill or be killed, and even though I'm out numbered, I won't go down without a fight.

I'm not sure who fires first, but Xavier and his friend don't have silencers, and the sound is deafening. A bullet wizzes by ear as I pull the trigger on my gun. The man in front of me drops, but he's still alive. He shoots his gun again at the same time I shoot mine, but my second shot is a headshot and kills him instantly, while his shot grazes the side of my boot.

I whirl around, gun still raised, to find that nobody else is in here. Xavier is gone.

Something catches my eye right outside the door. It's a foot, but not just any foot. It's Jasper's foot.

Gage and Silas come rushing in like a tidal wave.

"Come on, come on. We gotta hurry. People will be out here any second," Gage says hurriedly.

He passes me and goes to Jai at the table. My eyes are stuck on Jasper. His lifeless eyes stare up into the night sky.

"He's dead," I whisper, almost to myself, but Gage says the same thing.

"What?" Silas grits.

"Jai's dead," Gage responds. "We gotta go."

It takes a few seconds to click. "Jai's dead?" I ask.

"Yes, let's go," Gage responds, pushing me out of the shed.

I feel like I'm in a daze. Jasper's dead, because he was coming to help me save Jai. He must have found a way to jump the fence. Considering his height, a good jump could get him to the top. He did all of that to make sure I was okay, only to die.

Our mission to save Jai, was not only pointless because we were too late, but it also caused the death of another one of our own.

"Okay, just hold on," Silas whispers.

Taking note of where we are, I recognize the Lincoln we're crouching behind. Voices erupt from behind us, all of them making their way to the shed.

We slide around the back of the Lincoln, getting out of view from the people behind us, but trying not to be seen by the guards in front. Gun shots ring out somewhere near the front of the house, causing the guards to run in that direction.

"Now," Silas says.

We're up and running, going in the direction they came from when they first got here. The guards are distracted on the other side, making me wonder if it's our guys who's distracting them.

Before I know it, we're at the car, and Gage is speeding away. Silas texts everyone else, and as we wait for responses, tears run in steady streams down my cheeks.

# CHAPTER 7

LATER THAT NIGHT, I'M SANDWICHED in between Gage and Rem on the couch in our living room. I've finally stopped crying, for now anyway, and the guys' sadness has now turned into rage. Seeing grown men cry has always affected me, but seeing these men, my men, cry because we've lost members of our own kind of family has got to be the worst pain.

"Jai had a bullet wound to the head," Gage says between clenched teeth. "Do you think Xavier did that?"

"I don't know. Everything happened so fast. The only thing I'm sure of is that I killed the other guy."

"Do we know if Jai was dead before you went in there?" Silas asks. "Not that it makes too much a difference, I suppose."

"I didn't have time to check. I just assumed he was out of it. Where did you guys go when X and that other guy went to the shed? I thought you'd be close by when I went in."

"We weren't sure if we were going to be visible, so we went back up near the Lincoln. I'm sorry, C," Gage says.

I shrug. Who knows if it would have made a difference anyway?

"I'm going to assume X killed Jasper on his way out

of the shed," Silas adds. "We cannot let that mother fucker live."

"They're all going to be on high guard now. We've killed one of theirs on Roman's property. It's real now, and the bloodshed won't end until one of our crews has been extinguished completely," Gage states, his voice a low rumble of hatred and sorrow.

"Before we left tonight, I got ahold of Lou and told them to go ahead and start gathering who they could. We should be more prepared in a couple days," Silas announces. "We'll have more power behind us."

"Until then, we need to stay low. Stay here if we can," Gage adds.

I nod my head. "Everyone can stay here. The house is stocked up on everything we need." Pushing myself up, I say, "I'm going to bed."

"You need anything?" Gage asks

"Just sleep. Night, guys," I say as I pass them and slowly trudge up the stairs.

I pass Jasper's room, and the urge to open his door is too strong to ignore. When I walk inside, I'm greeted by his scent. Nothing too specific, just so clearly Jasper. His bed was left unmade, clothes strewn about the room. Condoms rest on the dresser next to jolly ranchers and cigarette packs.

I sit on the edge of his bed and run my hand over the sheets.

"I'm sorry, Jasper. I'm sorry I couldn't protect you, but thank you for coming to find me. You were looking out for me, and in the end it cost you your life. I promise to not let you go unavenged."

A few more tears trickle down my face as I say goodbye to my brother. He may not have been blood related, but we were all he had, and he was family we had chosen. I go to my own room and whisper more apologies to Jai. I ask him to forgive me, even though I know he can't hear me. I need to say it aloud for myself. I need to admit my guilt and try to move on. There isn't time to be depressed right now. Not being sharp will only cause more deaths, and if anyone else is to die, it's going to be the enemy.

The more I continue to replay what happened, the more enraged I get. Even though Xavier was sure to let me know he would do what he had to do, I guess there was a part of me that thought he wouldn't actually kill any of my friends. Once again, I was wrong.

Xavier seems to be Roman's attack dog. Roman has yet to show his face, but X is always front and center. He needs to go.

My memories and thoughts of Xavier follow me into my dreams, and I remember my second encounter with the devilishly handsome and scarily intense Xavier Delgado.

***Past***

*"Wow, look at that one! That's a good prospect. Big, but not too big."*

*"Lee, I can't believe we're having this conversation. Do you understand what you're talking about right now?" I ask, bewildered.*

*"Of course I know! I'm trying to pick out a nice guy for you to lose your virginity to! You don't want them to be too big, in case they're . . . too big. You know? However, some guys might surprise you. He's cute, looks gentle enough. I say go for him."*

*I slap my hand on my forehead. "What am I supposed to say? Oh hey, excuse me, I'm looking to lose my virginity, and you look gentle enough. Wanna have sex with me?"*

*"No," she drags out, "you say, hey, want a blowjob? And then it'll go from there."*

*We both bust out laughing at the table. A few people nearby give us a strange look, but for the most part, the loud music in the club drowns us out. The bright green wristbands we're forced to wear alert everyone that we're underage, but we're just happy to be able to get into a club.*

*"So, you gonna talk to that guy or what?" Lee asks.*

*"Probably not, Lee. As cliché as it may sound, I kind of want my first time to mean something. At least a little something. More than me just doing it to get it over with."*

*"Well, I'm no pro, myself. I've only been with one guy, but we did it like three times," she says, twirling a piece of hair around her finger. "You got anybody special in mind?" she asks, leaning forward with a sparkle in her eye. "Maybe someone named Xavier?"*

*I roll my eyes, but I can't hide the smile that forms on my face. "Oh whatever. He's much older than me, and he probably wouldn't even look at me in that way," I say, really hoping and wishing that he could see me as a woman and not a girl.*

*"I wouldn't say much older. Six years isn't a lot, and you're eighteen now. Legal. Legal is good. Plus, you don't have a typical teen body. Your boobs are huge, and that screams womanly. You have a nice curve to your hips. Men love that shit."*

*I shrug it off. "I haven't seen him in a while, anyway. I won't hold my breath on that dream."*

*I take a sip of my non-alcoholic drink, and notice Lee's gone quiet. When I look up at her, she's looking past me, moving her head from side to side like she's trying to look for someone. I turn in my chair, but all I can see is a crowd of bodies either dancing or standing around and talking.*

*"What are you looking at?" I finally ask.*

*"Well, Chelle, I'm thinkin' a while has come to an end."*

*"What?"*

*"I'm pretty sure I just saw Xavier. Not positive, though, but really, how can you mistake him for anyone else?"*

*Turning in my seat once again, I try to scan the crowd for the face I've come to memorize. My heart races in excitement and nervousness. If I see him, what would I say? "Hey, I'm legal now!" Maybe, if he could just see me in this form fitting dress that has my boobs and curves on display, he'll be able to think of me as something more than Memphis' kid. Maybe he'll come to me and speak first, unable to ignore me. Then again, maybe that's just wishful thinking on my part.*

*"I have an idea!" Lee exclaims.*

*She pulls me by the hand and drags me to the elevated dance floor. It sits a few steps higher than the larger dance floor, and has bright lights along the back.*

*"Good idea!" I say, understanding her plan.*

*If Xavier is here, he'll have a better chance at seeing me up here.*

*Lee and I balance on our high heels and dance to the rhythmic beats of the music. Our bodies move seductively, gaining attention from some guys nearby. I try to look out into the crowd, but even at this level, it's hard to see.*

*After a few songs, Lee and I are both tired and sweaty. We shrug in defeat and make our way off the stage.*

*"Bathroom?" Lee mouths.*

*I nod and follow behind her. A group of drunk girls push through us and I lose sight of Lee. Continuing my journey to the bathroom, I walk down a slight ramp and look around for the bathroom. A small alcove to the right of me holds an ATM and the men's bathroom just past it, while the female bathroom is straight ahead.*

*As I'm passing the ATM, a sultry voice penetrates my eardrums.*

*"Well, look who it is."*

*I turn to the right and see Xavier standing near the men's bathroom.*

*"Xavier." My breath is so soft and airy that I'm sure he doesn't hear me.*

*He crooks his finger, calling me towards him. I inhale*

*deeply through my nose and tell myself this is my chance to show him the sexy side of me. Not that I'm too familiar with being sexy, but tonight, in these clothes and makeup, I feel sexy. My hair is parted on the side and pulled over one shoulder, falling in waves. Thank goodness for a good hair day today.*

*I walk slowly, one foot in front of the other, causing my hips to sway. My back is erect and my head held high. The strapless, black dress hugs my body and stops above my knees. Xavier's eyes look me up and down in the most obvious way.*

*Stopping a couple of feet away from him, I give him what I think is my most seductive smile.*

*"Xavier," I say in greeting. "Nice to see you again."*

*"Yes, it's been a little while, hasn't it?" His eyes drink me in. "You're looking good."*

*"Thank you."*

*"So, are you trying to get the attention of every man in here?" One brow lifts up in question.*

*"Not every man, no," I answer.*

*One corner of his mouth lifts in response. "Happy belated birthday," he says.*

*"You remembered."*

*"Of course. You were only a week from being eighteen when I saw you last, and it's been a few months now."*

*"Right, well, thank you."*

*"Done anything to celebrate your legal age? Buy cigarettes? Porn, maybe?"*

*I roll my eyes. "No, haven't done either of those, yet."*

*He smiles. "You're a good girl." The way he says it sounds almost accusatory.*

*Narrowing my eyes at him, I say, "I suppose that's a bad thing to you? I'll have you know, I'm not as good as you might think."*

*"Oh yeah? Tell me how bad you've been," he says, coming closer to me. His voice is a low husky tone.*

*I lick my lips. "I got a tattoo, and a piercing. I'm also here when I'm not supposed to be," I reply.*

*Xavier raises both brows and grins in amusement. "Wow, what a bad girl you are," he responds, mocking me.*

*"You're an asshole. You know damn well I'm not some innocent and naïve girl. I know what my dad and the guys do. I'm exposed to drugs, alcohol, and violence. None of those things bother me. Excuse me for not buying porn and cigarettes, but both are readily available at my house if I wanted them. I know how to shoot a gun, and I know how to defend myself. I also know a giant prick when I see one, so excuse me, I'll be leaving."*

*With anger and embarrassment running through me, I turn and start towards the bathroom. I can't believe what an asshole he is. This whole time I've been lusting after him and crushing on him from afar, not knowing he was a dick. My virginity is the only innocent thing about me. He should know I'm not frightened by their lifestyle. If anything, you'd think he'd be happy to have a girl who isn't going to run scared.*

*"Do you?" his voice calls out.*

*I turn around with a scowl on my face. "What?"*

*"Do you really know a giant prick when you see one?" he asks as he grabs himself for a brief second.*

*My eyes widen momentarily, but then I pull myself together. "Yes, and I also know when not to waste my time." I move my gaze to his crotch then up to his face and shrug.*

*When I get to the bathroom, I see Lee standing there with wide eyes.*

*"Oh my gosh," she mouths.*

*I pull her into the bathroom.*

*"Did you hear?" I ask.*

*"Yes! What in the actual fuck?"*

*"He's an asshole, that's what. What a waste."*

*"I'd still do him."*

*I shake my head and go into the stall. When I come out and wash my hands, Lee is still looking at me in surprise.*

*"What?" I snap.*

*"I'm just surprised you said that to him. You've been in love with him forever."*

*With a roll of my eyes, I say, "I'm not in love. Can we go now?"*

*"Yeah."*

*Lee and I walk quickly through the club and finally emerge into the clear, night air. The breeze feels good on my skin, and I lift my hair off my neck and enjoy the coolness as the wind hits the sweat that rests there.*

*"Chevelley," a deep voice says from behind.*

*Both Lee and I turn to see Xavier standing there, leaning against the front of the building, smoking a cigarette.*

*"Uhh. I'm gonna go wait in the car," Lee announces. She pulls me around to face her. "Don't let him leave without wanting to see you again," she whispers through a clenched jaw. "Bye, Xavier!" she calls before walking off.*

*"What do you want?" I say in clipped words.*

*A few club patrons stumble out, laughing and holding on to each other. Xavier cocks his head, telling me to follow him. With a quick look in Lee's direction, I hold up a finger and follow Xavier to the side of the building.*

*"I'm sorry if I hurt your feelings earlier."*

*"You didn't hurt my feelings. You just pissed me off."*

*He laughs a short laugh. "Fair enough. I'm sorry for pissing you off."*

*"Okay. Is that all?"*

*"No." He takes a slow drag of his cigarette and blows the smoke up into the air. "I know you aren't naïve, but I also know you have an innocence to you. I'm not saying it's a bad thing, but it's the truth. Is it not?"*

*"What are you getting at?" I demand, not wanting to talk about the innocence I have. How would he know anyway?*

*"What I'm getting at is," he throws the cigarette and backs*

*me into the wall, "I want to steal that innocence from you. I want it to be mine."*

*Words fail me at this point. His body is pushed up against mine and his hand grazes my cheek and down my neck. My breathing escalates, causing my chest to rub against his. I lick my lips as I watch his mouth, wondering if he's going to kiss me or not.*

*"So, tell me. Will it be mine?" he whispers, his eyes looking down into mine.*

*I nod my head, but he inclines his head in a way that tells me he wants words. "Y-yes."*

*"Good, because I want you to be my good girl and my bad girl. Got it? Will you wait for me?"*

*"Wait?" I ask shakily. "Wait till when?"*

*A look passes over his features. Sadness? Apprehension? I can't tell.*

*"Just wait," he says softly.*

*Before I can respond, his mouth touches mine. His kisses are soft and slow at first. I bring my hands to his waist and grip the black shirt in my fists, pulling him closer. I feel his large hand grab the back of my neck right before his tongue probes my lips and enters the warmth of my mouth.*

*Our tongues dance sensually together, and it's a dance I never want to end. I've kissed a couple of boys before, but they were novices compared to Xavier. I feel a warmth and heaviness in my lower stomach. I squeeze my thighs together as his hands roam my body, wetness gathering between my legs*

*Maybe realizing that any more of this could lead to public indecency, he pulls away slowly, giving me small pecks on my lips before disentangling himself altogether.*

*"I've wanted to do that for a while now," he breathes.*

*"Yeah?" I ask, the glee clear in my tone.*

*"Yeah," he replies with a smile.*

*"When will I see you again?" I ask.*

*He looks off to the side. "I'm not sure, but as soon as I can,*

*I'm gonna come find you, okay?" He turns back and looks me straight in the eye. "Remember what I said."*

*"Okay."*

*He walks me back to Lee's car, gives me a quick peck, and then he disappears into the night.*

*I don't see Xavier for another six months.*

# CHAPTER 8

I WAKE IN THE MIDDLE of the night, drenched in sweat and tears. I dreamt of Jasper, Jai, and Xavier. My body trembles with anger and overwhelming despair. I allow the anger to takeover, because I can deal with that easier than I can the sadness. Against better judgment—and perhaps without much thought at all—I climb out of bed, throw on some jeans and a T-shirt, grab my gun, and leave the house.

Grief, guilt, and ire fuel me. I go to the only place that even came to mind. Xavier's. His modest house is very familiar to me. Spending many of my nights with him several years ago still feels like it was just recently. The memories are ingrained into my brain, leaving me unable to forget about him. About who he used to be, anyway.

Xavier is nothing like the man I thought I once loved. Xavier is now a cruel, ruthless bastard who's killed my friends, and that's why I know without a shadow of a doubt, that I have to kill him. If he lives any longer he'll only take more people that I love away from me. It hurts to know that's the truth, since he knows I don't have any family. Perhaps he wants me to be like him.

It should be easy to sneak into his unguarded home, get into his bedroom, and shoot him before he wakes. I know the layout of his house like the back of my hand. There will be no need to turn on lights and fumble around.

I step out of my car and close the door as quietly as possible. I'm parked a half a block away, so it doesn't take me long to reach the front of his house. It's bathed in darkness, but I know he's here. Xavier's always loved being in the comfort of his own home.

After a glance in the front window, I know he's not downstairs, but I also know his front door holds three different locks. I go to the rear of the house and walk straight to the window that leads to his laundry room. It's a fairly narrow window, and it's the only one that doesn't have a lock on it, but I know I'll be able to fit through it. I once had to sneak out the same window when my dad had come over.

It takes a few hard pushes to get the window to open, and as much as I was hoping it would open quietly, I'm not so lucky. The window clearly never gets used, because a loud pop followed by a drawn out creak fills the silent night as I finally get it open. Waiting outside for a minute, I pause, listening for footsteps coming down the stairs to investigate.

When I'm sure he's still asleep, I lift myself up, the palms of my hands digging into the track of the window, and get in as noiselessly as I can. The laundry room is small and dark, but the door is only a few steps away.

With my heart in my throat, I put my hand on the doorknob and turn it as slow as possible. I'm met with a view of the kitchen, everything spotlessly clean like usual. I turn to the left, knowing the stairs aren't far away, and begin my journey to Xavier's room. Once at the top, I travel down the short hall and make a left.

His door is more than halfway closed, giving me just enough room to peek inside and see his motionless body on the bed. With a silent prayer that his door doesn't squeak, I push it open a little further as I step inside. My eyes never leave his sleeping form as I move to the nightstand next to him. I know he keeps his gun on the small table, so I take it and slide it underneath his bed.

Looking at his relaxed face, it's hard to believe he's capable of all the things he's done. He's so handsome, and easily could have been a model had he had taken a different path in life. I guess I can't judge too harshly, I'm no better than he.

I take my glock out and aim it directly at his forehead. A clean shot. Quick. Painless. A luxury Jai didn't get. With my finger on the hammer of the gun, I take a deep breath and say goodbye.

Instead of the sound of my gun going off, the shrieking sound of a phone fills the room. Without thought, I swiftly take four steps back and hide in the shadows of his bathroom. I hear him begin to stir and then his voice, rough with sleep, answers the phone.

"Yeah? At my house. Really? Okay, well was everything at Roman's taken care of? Uh-huh. Okay, good. No, I'm not sure. I don't think that would happen. Okay. Bye."

I can't see Xavier from my hiding spot in the bathroom. Based on noise alone, I can tell he never moved from the bed while talking on the phone. I try to decipher what he could have been talking about through his side of the conversation, but it's impossible to know for sure.

The bed squeaks and my heart races. Is he getting out of the bed? Maybe he'll need to use the bathroom, and if so, there's no way I could continue to hide from him. I hold the gun tight in my hand, ready for anything.

Xavier sighs loudly, his voice no closer than it was before. I have no idea what time it is, but based on the time I left my house, it might be around four-thirty or five in the morning. I need to make sure I'm out of here before sun starts to come up.

I feel like I stand in the bathroom for fifteen minutes before I chance a look around the door and into the bedroom. His back is towards me as he sleeps on his side, so I figure now is a better time than any to make my escape. Grateful that I put on my hoodie in the car, I pull the hood over my head, and take slow and cautious steps as I re-enter the shadowy bedroom.

A couple of feet from his bed, I take aim once again and cock the gun. The sound seems to echo loudly through the room. Suddenly and without warning, Xavier's body whirls around with the gun that I had put under the bed now pointed at me.

I don't think. I shoot and then I run. A bullet imbeds itself into the door as I'm running out. I stretch my hand out behind me as I step into the hall and fire one last shot in Xavier's direction. I run for my life—literally—rushing down the stairs and back into the laundry room where I launch myself out the window. I feel a sharp pain in my knee as I bang it roughly against the window pane, but I don't stop. I keep running until I reach my car and never look behind me.

As I'm whipping the car around to drive in the opposite direction of his house, I don't see any sign of him. I breathe a sigh of relief and make my way back home.

When I finally pull up to my house, I lean my head on the steering wheel and smack the dashboard with both hands.

"What the fuck are you doing, Chevelley?"

I chide myself for being so reckless and stupid. I'd get in anybody else's ass if they did the same thing. I let my emotions get the best of me, and it could have gotten me killed. Now I have to wait for word on Xavier and see if I shot him or not. If I didn't, and he got a good look at me, I know I just made this whole thing a lot worse. However, the thought of killing him makes me feel sick.

Creeping into my house as quietly as possible, I try to make it to my room without running into or waking anybody up. The last thing I need is someone questioning where I've been. Luckily, nobody is in the living room. Once upstairs, I open the door to my dark room, grateful that the sun isn't up just yet, and jump back into bed.

As I lay there, begging unconsciousness to take me, I'm transported back to when I was eighteen years old. When I finally saw Xavier again after six months of waiting for him.

***Past***

*"Yo, C! We're going to a party. Get dressed and be ready in ten minutes," Gage hollers from the living room.*

*I storm out of the kitchen. "Gage! You want me ready in ten minutes? I haven't even showered today. Why didn't you tell me earlier?"*

*"Not my fault you were a lazy ass today. Go take a shower, then. You have fifteen minutes."*

*I growl at him as I run up the stairs.*

*My plans for today were to lounge around in my sweats, eat junk food, and watch movies, but a party with the guys is always fun.*

*These guys around here don't understand that a girl needs more than ten minutes' notice to go somewhere. I'm not sure why they haven't figured that out yet. You'd think they'd tell me ahead of time, so they wouldn't have to wait on me.*

*I take the quickest shower possible, throw on some tight blue jeans that are frayed on the thigh, and a black Jack Daniels shirt that's been cut, exposing just a couple inches of my stomach, and some white Chucks finish the outfit. My black hair is thrown into a bun since I don't have time to do anything to it.*

*"Done!" I yell out when I get to the bottom of the stairs.*

*Gage opens the screen door directly in front of the stairs and pops his head in. "That was twenty minutes. Let's go."*

*"It's not my fault you tell me shit at the last minute. Twenty minutes might be a record. Where we going anyway?"*

*Gage slips behind the wheel of his old truck, and I sit in the middle while Silas slides into the passenger seat.*

*"A party at Jai's. There's probably gonna be a lot of people."*

*I don't question the party. Usually, we don't need reasons to have or go to parties. It's just something to do. I'm just grateful Gage invites me. I'm almost nineteen, but my dad is sure to let Gage know he's responsible for me once we step out of the house. If anything happens to me, I'm sure something would happen to Gage.*

*"Where's Dad?" I ask.*

*"Business."*

*Gage and Silas engage in conversation about some blonde chick with huge tits, and that's where I check out of the conversation. A little while later, we pull up to Jai's small house only to find we have to park down the block because of the amount of cars already parked near his place.*

*We walk right in when we get to the door, knowing even if we knocked, nobody would hear it. We have to push our way in through the mass of people.*

*Before I get very far in I hear a squeal and see a streak of blonde hair running at me.*

*"I'm so glad you're here!" Levi screeches.*

*"What's going on?" I ask. "Looks like the whole city is here."*

*"I know. It's crazy!"*

*Gage and Silas find Jai and Rem, while I go with Lee to where she had been sitting with some guy.*

*"Chevelley this is Jason. Jason, this is my best friend, Chevelley."*

*Jason turns and looks at me with small, dark eyes. "Chevelley, huh? That's a strange name."*

*"Jason, huh? That's a pretty common name."*

*His mouth twitches slightly, but he doesn't say anything else. I look at Lee and she just rolls her eyes.*

*"Anyway, so how long have you been here?" I ask.*

*"About an hour."*

*"And the man of the hour isn't even here yet," Jason chimes in.*

*"Man of the hour?" I question. "Is it somebody's birthday?"*

*Jason gives me a strange look like he's questioning why I'm here if I don't know who the party's for. "No. It's a coming home party."*

*"For?"*

*"For Xavier."*

*My wide eyes find Lee's. The fact that hers are just as wide tell me she had no idea either. She quickly stands and pulls me by my arm, both of us rushing outside where there are fewer people.*

*"C, I had no idea! Jason asked if I wanted to go to a party, and I said sure! I didn't know it was for X."*

*"Holy shit. Did he say a coming home party? Where's he been this whole time?"*

*"I don't know. You know there were a few rumors going around."*

*I nod my head. About a month after Xavier had been gone, people started saying he got caught up in some bad shit and had to go into hiding. Others said he had to go to jail, and a few even said he was dead.*

*Just like mine, Xavier's dad is involved in underground business. Business that isn't exactly safe or legal. His dad's business dealings are with guns and gangs. Xavier's been working with him for a little while, by being the go between with the gangs and gun dealers. It's definitely not a job I'd want. You get a lot of pissed off gang bangers, and a lot of pissed off dealers if they aren't paid what they're owed.*

*"Well . . . shit."*

*Lee laughs. "Wanna sneak a shot or two? Gage probably won't even see us."*

*"Yeah, let's go."*

*Lee and I get to the kitchen and find a lot of empty liquor bottles strewn about the counter and thrown in the sink. There's a big bottle of Bacardi Gold left, so we settle for that. We can't find shot glasses, so we just pour what we assume is two shots' worth of liquor in our plastic cups.*

*"To reunions?" Lee asks, her cup in the air.*

*I scrunch up my nose. "Uh. To drinking?"*

*We laugh and drink half the Bacardi from the cup.*

*"C! What are you drinking?" Gage's voice shouts from the other side of the kitchen.*

*"What?" I ask dumbly as he gets closer.*

*He takes my cup and sniffs. "What's this shit?"*

*"Umm . . ."*

*"Cut the shit. You think I don't know you drink? I'm not stupid. Just don't drink too much. You can't be drunk here. I can't have guys trying to take advantage of you, and I really don't want to deal with your dad either. That's all you get," he says, handing the cup back to me.*

*"Thanks."*

*Gage walks off and Lee begins laughing. "I always thought we were so slick."*

*"Apparently not."*

*"Okay, well, let's finish this nasty shit."*

*We gulp down the rest of our drinks and then swipe some sodas from the fridge for a chaser.*

*"I got a joint. Wanna sneak out back?" Lee asks with mischief in her eyes.*

*"You know, you're a bad influence. You have your parents fooled, don't you?" I say with a smile.*

*Her face transforms to one full of innocence and naivety. She bats her eyelashes over her large eyes. "I don't know what you're talking about, momma. I've never smoked weed in my life. I don't even know what it looks like. It must be Justin's," she says in a cutesy voice as she twirls her hair.*

*"Did you really blame your brother?" I laugh.*

*Back to her "normal" voice, she says, "Well, in my defense, it could have been his. Mom found a baggy in the car. Either one of us could have dropped it. It doesn't matter that I had been searching for the baggy I had lost earlier in the day," she says with a wink.*

*"You're something else."*

*"I know, but you also know you want to come. So, let's hurry before big brother Gage comes back."*

*We rush to the back door and are relieved to find that nobody is outside. Lee lights up the joint and takes a hit before passing it to me. It doesn't take long to finish it, but as I'm taking the last hit, we hear footsteps coming from the side of the house.*

*I hurriedly blow out the smoke and toss the joint in the grass. Xavier rounds the corner and my heart and stomach both do flips.*

*He looks surprised to see us out here, but he adjusts his face quickly and gives us a small smile.*

*"Wasn't expecting anybody to be back here," he says.*

*"Neither were we," Lee replies.*

*"I can tell. You know weed has a very distinct smell. Can't really get rid of that."*

*Xavier walks up two of the three stairs that lead to the little landing we're on. When he looks up at me, I want to wrap my arms around his neck and kiss him until my tongue is sore. But I don't.*

*"Well, Xavier it's nice to see you again. I'm glad you're*

*alive and well, but I'm gonna head inside real quick. C, come find me in a bit."*

*I nod and smile at Lee and then it's just me and X.*

*The silence looms for a while. Neither of us sure of what to say, perhaps. I want to ask where he's been, but maybe it's too soon. Maybe it's none of my business. If he wants me to know, he'll tell me. I say the only thing I can think of.*

*"I waited."*

*It takes only a second before realization dawns on his face. One side of his mouth lifts.*

*"Oh yeah?"*

*Afraid my voice will fail me, I only nod.*

*"It's been a while." He says it like he doesn't believe I could have waited six months.*

*"I know."*

*"Do you want to ask where I've been? What I've been up to? Or do you know?"*

*"No, I don't know. I heard rumors. If you want to clear those up, you can."*

*He grunts in amusement. "Rumors. I can only imagine. When can I see you again?" he asks. "Alone."*

*"When do you want to?" I question.*

*"Now," he growls, taking the last step to get to me. He towers over me, and runs the pad of his thumb over my bottom lip.*

*"But, people are waiting on you inside," I say softly.*

*"You've been waiting on me for six months."*

*His mouth connects to mine and my body melts into him. He wraps his arms around me and brings me in close. Even though we've only kissed once before, it's like our mouths remember each other. It's familiar and it's intoxicating.*

*We hear the door begin to open and pull away from each other hastily. A guy I don't recognize comes out.*

*"Holy shit! X, man. I didn't know you were here." He turns and shouts into the house. "Xavier's here! Get him a*

*drink!"*

*He pulls X into one of those man handshakes slash hugs and then walks back into the house. He's waiting for Xavier to follow him, so I know my time with him is over.*

*Xavier leans close to me. "Tomorrow. I'll meet you outside your place tomorrow night at six. Come up with an excuse to be gone all night."*

*I nod twice and then Xavier is pulled into the house and cheers erupt. Everybody seems happy to have him back, but nobody could be happier than me.*

# CHAPTER 9

I EXPECT THERE TO BE chaos when I get downstairs. I can only imagine that if Xavier is still alive, he told Roman what happened. When word gets out that someone tried to kill Xavier, or if he's dead and people have found out, Roman will know it was one of us. There will be hell to pay, and I almost regret going over there in the first place, but I don't. Fuck that and fuck him. He killed my friends. My family. For that alone, he deserves to die.

Instead, what I find downstairs is almost unsettling. It's quiet and calm with nobody anywhere to be found. There's always someone here, so the fact that the house is empty makes me worry. I make a cup of coffee before I venture out back. When I get outside, I can see that the door to our shed is slightly open.

I'm wearing jeans, a shirt that falls off one shoulder, and socks. I didn't bother with shoes, but now that I'm walking over dampened grass, I regret not putting on slippers or something. As I near the door, I hear low voices talking amongst themselves. I pull open the door and slip in to find some guy lying on the floor and Gage and Silas standing near him.

"What the hell is going on?" I ask, grabbing their attention.

When Gage looks back at me, he looks pissed. Silas looks more worried than anything.

"This fucking guy was trying to get over our fence. I saw him when I went out to get something from my truck. After a bit of a fight, I knocked him out and Silas came and helped me get him in here."

Gage rubs his hand over his mouth where it's obvious the unconscious man got a good hit at him. His lip is cut and blood is already starting to dry around it.

"Did he have the chance to say anything?" I ask.

"He was trying to say he followed someone here early this morning. I don't know what the hell he was talking about, but I'll find out soon enough."

Gage grabs a thick piece of rope from the corner and ties the man's hands behind his back before roughly pulling his body to a sitting position and placing him against the wall. All I can think about is that this guy was watching Xavier's house and saw me leave, following me home. Fuck.

Gage starts smacking the man in the face, bringing him to consciousness. Silas looks over his shoulder at me, and something in his eyes tells me he knows something. I have a feeling it's something I don't want him to know. The fact that he's not saying anything tells me he doesn't want Gage to know.

The man begins to groan, gaining all of our attention. His eyes flicker open and when he takes in his surroundings, he tries to get up and move, but Gage puts his boot on the man's chest, preventing him from getting up.

"I don't think so. What the fuck were you doing trying to get over our fence? Who are you?"

He looks at all three of us, and actually looks a little nervous, but he doesn't respond at all to Gage's questions.

"You hear me fucking talking to you?" Gage spits.

"What're you doing here, huh? Who you lookin' for?"

The man spits out a mixture of saliva and blood on Gage's boot which sets Gage off. He pulls the man up by his shirt and shoves him against the wall.

"You're gonna tell me what the fuck you were trying to do here, or you're going to fucking die. Do you understand that?"

"I told you," the man grunts. "I followed someone here." He spits again, but this time wisely aims away from Gage.

"That doesn't tell me anything. Is someone else here?"

He shrugs. "Don't know."

Gage cocks his arm back like he's gonna punch the guy, but Silas steps in.

"Come on, man. Let me talk to him."

Silas pulls Gage away, knowing Gage is capable of losing his cool and beating this guy until he isn't able to say anything.

"You followed someone here?" Silas asks. "But, you don't know this person?"

"Nah, I don't know them. I saw them around my boss' house, and I followed them here."

My heart drops. He saw me.

"And who's your boss?" Gage demands.

The man's eyes look to mine and then back to Silas. He ignores Gage altogether. "I think you know."

"Roman?" Silas asks.

"Look, I wasn't sent here. I came here because someone from this house was somewhere they shouldn't be. Anybody from here should know to stay far away." Once again, he makes sure to make eye contact with me.

Xavier's words come back to me. *Stay as far away from me as possible. I mean it. You're going to get yourself killed.*

Nobody else knows he told me that. Gage and Silas

wouldn't know Xavier was trying to send me a message, which is exactly what this guy is doing. Xavier is still alive and he sent this guy here to let me know.

"Nobody was anywhere near Roman last night, so I don't know what the fuck you're talking about. I think you're full of shit and have another reason for being here. We should kill you right fucking now, you piece of shit!" Gage yells, leaning over Silas' shoulder and getting in the guy's face.

I know I should be questioning this guy. I know that by sitting back quietly, I might look weak or guilty, but that's how I feel. I am guilty. I shouldn't have been at Xavier's house, but my grief and anger took over. This guy knows it was me that was there, and that means Xavier knows it was me. I need to tell Gage and Silas the truth. They're going to be pissed, but I can't lie to them, especially if my actions have already started more drama.

"He followed me."

Three pairs of eyes look at me and the room goes silent.

"What?" Gage grits between his teeth.

Silas gives me a small shake of his head like he's telling me I shouldn't have told Gage, but he doesn't say anything. Maybe he saw me leave or saw me come home and I didn't realize.

"I left last night, or early this morning, I guess. I was just so angry and so upset that I had to get out. I drove around and ended up driving near Xavier's house."

"What the fuck were you thinking?" Gage yells. "You know better than that, C! What the hell?"

"I wasn't fucking thinking, okay?" I yell.

"It's fine. She drove around. That doesn't mean anything. I mean, it's stupid, but she didn't do anything," Silas says. "It brought this fucking guy here, but I can understand why he followed her back if she was lurking around Xavier's house."

I open my mouth to tell them the truth, but the look Silas gives me with the slight shake of his head tells me to keep quiet.

When I look at the other guy, he gives me a smirk, letting me know he knows it was more than me driving around, too.

"Well, now you know who it was, and you know nothing happened. She was angry, as we all are," Silas tells the man. "Maybe she thought about doing something stupid, but she didn't. If we let you go, you better not come back."

The man only gives the smallest nod in acknowledgment, but Silas grabs his arm and pushes him out of the shed and all the way to the front of the house. It isn't until we get out the front gate that he undoes the rope from the guy's wrists. Gage stays back, leaning on his truck and watching us from afar. I can tell his pissed at me, but I'll have to deal with his wrath later.

"Like I said, don't come back here," Silas threatens.

"I won't have a need to as long as other people don't go where they aren't supposed to," he says, piercing me with his eyes. "You're lucky it was me who saw you and nobody else."

"What the fuck is that supposed to mean?" I ask.

He puts his hands in his back pockets and gives me a creepy grin before stepping right up to me. He leans in like he's going to tell me something in my ear, then I feel his hand on my ass.

"Be smart," he whispers.

"Alright, mother fucker," Silas says right as I push the man away from me.

"Keep your fucking hands off me!"

His response is to smile and then walk down the

street. Silas and I stand there until we can't see him anymore.

"You were gone for an awful long time to have just driven by his house and come back," Silas states.

"I know."

"Gage is already pissed. He doesn't need to know much more right now, but you need to make better decisions. I think your past with X is the only reason why you're still alive. Had it have been any of us at his house last night, we would be dead."

"Xavier doesn't have any feelings for me. He's already threatened my life. I just got lucky."

Silas grunts. "Exchange the word lucky with pussy, and you got it right."

"Shut up. How did you know I was gone, anyway?" I ask.

"I couldn't sleep. I was outside in my car."

He doesn't have to say anything else. The look on his face tells me he was dealing with his emotions in private. I don't respond, and we walk back into the house together. I don't bother approaching Gage. He'll come to me when he's calmed down.

When I get to my bedroom, my phone is ringing on my dresser. A quick look at the caller ID tells me it's Lou.

"Hey, Lou. What's up?"

"We have Mario Ambrossi and two people from the Muccino family here. The Carters have their own shit going on, so they probably won't make it," Lou says, getting straight to the point. "Mario knows Roman, and he's gonna call him up and set up a meeting telling him he wants guns. The Muccino brothers are going to find a way to get to Roman's car and plant an explosive."

"Okay, and when is this meeting going to take place?" I inquire.

"Soon. Mario's setting it up now. Once he has a

location, he'll inform us, and we'll have a few of our people near the spot. Roman and his driver will leave the location, and I'm sure he'll leave a few of his guys behind. I have no doubt it'll be at one of his businesses after hours. So, we'll need our guys to get in that building around the time Roman's leaving, so that when his car explodes, we can take out the part of his crew that's there. Without a leader, and half a gang, the others won't know what to do. It should end things there."

"Sounds too easy."

"It won't be, that's for sure."

I sigh. "Alright, Lou. Let me know when we have a location and date. I'll inform everybody else."

"Will do. Be safe.

I go to slip the phone in my back pocket and hear a crinkling sound. Slipping my hand into my pocket, I feel a piece of paper and bring it out to look at.

It's a note with only a few words scrawled across it.

*Tomorrow. 6pm. We need to talk. Rec Center.*

The rec center in Overbrook Park. A place where me and Xavier would go all the time.

Shit.

# CHAPTER 10

GAGE CONTINUES TO IGNORE ME, but it's probably for the best. He needs to calm down. Rem, Trax, and Deacon come over, and I tell them all about my conversation with Lou. All I'm doing now is waiting for the final word on when and where, and hopefully we can end this before any more of our people die.

I'm also trying to figure out what the hell to do about Xavier. He wants to meet me, but I don't know if I can trust him. While he says we need to "talk" he could very well mean he needs to kill me. Of course there's the stupid part of my brain that's telling me to meet him and see what he has to say. Maybe he can provide me with some useful information about Roman.

If I tell any of the guys where I'm going and who I'm going to meet, they will either keep me from going or tag along and that will definitely not end well. I hate keeping stuff from them, but this is my crew and my decision. If Xavier wanted them in on a meeting, he would make that clear. The fact that his creepy friend slipped a note in my pocket tells me it was meant to be a secret meeting between the two of us. By going alone, am I keeping my crew safe? Or making it easy for me to go missing and have no one know what happened?

*Tomorrow night at 6.*

Familiar words from the same man, but that meeting years ago was much different.

***Past***

*"Do you know where he's taking you?" Lee asks, basically jumping up and down.*

*"No. He just told me to meet him outside and have an excuse to be gone all night. And, that's why you're here," I say with a smile.*

*"You're lucky you have an awesome best friend. So, you're 'spending the night at my house' right?"*

*"Yep That's what I'm gonna tell my dad."*

*"Well, I'll be expecting all the details," she says, waggling her brows. "So, did he tell you where he's been? Was he on the run?"*

*I shake my head while I rummage through my clothes. "He didn't say, but I didn't ask. Maybe I'll find out tonight."*

*"Makes sense to know what he's been up to. What if he was shackin' it up with some bimbo?"*

*"Then I'll have to kill him," I joke. "But really, I doubt it was that."*

*Levi gasps dramatically. "What if he has a wife and family somewhere else? Oh my gosh! I'll kill him!"*

*"Oh my God, calm down!" I say through laughter. "You're getting mad at him and you don't even know if it's necessary."*

*She shrugs and blows it off. "Anyway, your dad looked pissed when I came over. What's going on?"*

*"Same old shit," I say, lifting one shoulder. I show a shirt to Lee, but she scrunches up her face, so I throw it on the floor and look for something else. "He has a client who's trying to secure this building for his business, but somebody else is offering a full cash payment, even though his client supposedly closed the deal already. The other offer is from some mob guy, so I think the owner is gonna take his money just so he doesn't*

*get killed. Something like that."*

*"I don't understand all this shit."*

*"It gets confusing sometimes. Dad's client has his own beef with the mob guy, so it's getting messy. You know his clients aren't on the up and up, anyway."*

*She nods her head. "You're really gonna be in on all this?"*

*"It's all I know, Lee."*

*"I know," she says softly. "I just don't want you to get hurt . . . or worse."*

*"I'll be fine. Gage takes me shooting every weekend, and my dad enrolled me in self-defense classes when I was twelve."*

*She opens her mouth to say something, but I don't want to get in the conversation of what I'm doing with my life again, so I cut her off with a question about clothes.*

*"I really need your help finding something to wear. Do I go casual? Dress it up a bit? I don't know what to do!"*

*Lee rolls her eyes and gets up from the bed. "You're so bad at this getting dressed thing."*

*"Shut up," I say without malice. She's right. Levi is definitely more into fashion than I am. I go for comfort and not for style. She's the opposite.*

*Lee begins going through my clothes, so I flop onto the bed. "I wonder what we're gonna do."*

*Lee sticks her head out of the closet and says, "Have sex."*

*I roll over and stare at the ceiling above my bed. "Well, I'd hope so, but there has to be more, right? Otherwise, I'd just be a booty call."*

*"It better be more than that," Lee calls from the closet. "He's older, I'm sure he'll take you to dinner or something."*

*I sigh, but don't respond. I've been waiting for this day for a long time. The nerves have been in place all day. I can't tell you how many times I've imagined and fantasized about the day Xavier came back. It was hard waiting for him. I mean, hell, I'm fucking nineteen! All of my friends are having sex. I did have this guy friend, but we didn't do more than kissing and touching each other. I can only hope that while I was torturing myself waiting for Xavier that he wasn't out having all the sex in the world.*

*Gage overheard me and Lee talking about Xavier once, and was sure to try to scare me away from him. He said he wasn't somebody I should get involved with. We had one of the biggest fights we've ever had. I told him he has balls to judge someone else for what they do when this whole house is full of people who make a living by breaking the law. I called him a hypocrite, and then begged him not to tell my father. As far as I know, he hasn't. Dad hasn't said anything to me about it, but I question who my father expects me to fall for. Does he think I can bring home a police officer or a lawyer as a boyfriend? That would never happen. I'm bound to be with someone who lives the same lifestyle I do.*

*But, now that Xavier is back in town, I'm sure Gage will be on my case about him again. Which is exactly why I have to try to keep whatever this thing between X and I is, from Gage and everybody else.*

*"Okay, here," Lee says, throwing some clothes on top of me. "It's casual but cute. Not too fancy, because Xavier doesn't seem like the fancy schmancy type anyway."*

*I sit up and inspect the clothes. It's a pair of black leggings that look like they're leather, but it's definitely pleather. A long, white tank top, and a black blazer. Wait. Black blazer?*

*"I don't own a blazer."*

*"I know. I must have left it here, but it'll dress the outfit up a bit if you go out. Then you can take it off later."*

*I shrug. "Okay."*

*"Wear heels and not your Chucks."*

*"I wasn't gonna wear them anyway," I say, even though I did think about it.*

*"Good. Not on the first date. I'll put them in your overnight bag with something more comfortable to wear tomorrow. You might want to wear loose pants," she says with a*

*giggle.*

*Time flies as I change and begin doing my hair and makeup. And by "doing my hair and makeup" I mean, Lee taking over and doing it for me.*

*I end up with wavy hair that falls over my shoulders, and a semi-nude lip color with gloss to "accentuate my full lips" as Lee says, and some eyeliner and mascara.*

*At five-fifty, Lee and I go downstairs to face my dad before leaving.*

*"Daddy!" I call out in an innocent voice.*

*Lee rolls her eyes. "You can't be me."*

*"Watch me."*

*"Yeah, baby girl?"*

*My dad walks into the living room looking big and intimidating, but he's never really scared me. He's six foot three, two hundred and fifty pounds, and has a short beard that covers a ruggedly handsome face. His arms are covered in tattoos, the ink fading since he's had them since he was a teen.*

*"Lee and I are going out for a bit, and then I was wondering if I could stay the night at her house."*

*I give him a sweet smile and he looks both of us over. Lee dressed up too, so it wouldn't look weird with me being dressed to go out and not her.*

*"Where are you going?" he asks as he crosses his arms over his chest.*

*I panic for a split second, because I stupidly didn't think of this ahead of time.*

*"Well, Lee's brother invited us to this birthday party his friend is having. It's at Chino's and then we were gonna go back to finish celebrating at Lee's."*

*Dad grunts. "Chino's, huh?" He looks to Lee who stands there looking like the epitome of innocence. Her cherub face and big green eyes stare back at him. "I trust your brother will make sure you both stay safe."*

*She nods. "Of course, Mr. Reed. He's pretty protective.*

*I almost hate him for it, but hey, brothers," she says with a shrug.*

*"Well, okay. Just be careful. Call me later tonight."*

*"Thanks, Daddy!" I squeal as I wrap my arms around his neck. He hugs me back and lets out a rare chuckle.*

*"Yeah, yeah. Don't let any of those guys mess with you. You have your . . . uhh . . ."*

*"Daddy!" I screech.*

*"What? I was gonna say pepper spray."*

*The mischief in his eyes tell me that's not what he was gonna say. He knows I carry my compact, pocket pistol with me, but Lee freaks out around guns.*

*"Yes, I have my . . . pepper spray."*

*"Good."*

*"I love you."*

*"Love you, too, baby girl. Y'all be good."*

*"Always, Mr. Reed," Lee answers.*

*Dad scoffs. "Right." Then he walks away.*

*"I almost feel bad lying to him," Lee says.*

*"Me too. But, he doesn't need to know what's really happening tonight. I'm protecting him."*

*We laugh as we head outside.*

*Once we're out the gate and heading towards Lee's car that's parked along the curb, I see headlights come on from a little further down the street and the car begins to approach slowly.*

*My stomach is instantly in knots. Excitement and nervousness fight for who takes over, but I think excitement wins by just a tad. Lee stands near her car door, and we both wait until Xavier's black muscle car stops next to hers.*

*It's an old Camaro, but it's been upgraded in some areas, and the windows are so dark you can't see inside. Slowly, the window rolls down and I get a glimpse of his beautiful face. He gives me a small smile and jerks his head in a way that tells me to get in.*

*"Lee," he says in both greeting and dismissal to Levi.*

*She gives a small wave and then she and I say goodbye. I'm already sliding into the passenger seat as she's pulling off.*

*"You look absolutely beautiful," Xavier says right away. His smooth-as-honey voice gives me chills.*

*"Thank you," I reply.*

*"Are you hungry?"*

*I want to say that I'm starving for him, but figure I shouldn't. "I could eat," I say instead.*

*He chuckles. "I thought we could go eat and then . . ." he stops talking and looks in my direction. His brow is raised and he looks me over before turning his eyes back on the road.*

*"And then what?" I ask bravely.*

*"You know what."*

*"And where would we be going?"*

*"My house, of course."*

*The fact that he's six years older than me keeps slipping my mind. Of course he lives on his own. Plus, he makes money doing whatever he does for his dad's business, and I have no doubt his dad has plenty of money.*

*"Okay," I respond.*

*I stay quiet for a while, unsure of what to talk about. All I can think about is what's gonna happen when we get to his house.*

*"Chevelley."*

*His accented voice pierces through my thoughts. "Hmm?"*

*"Are you nervous around me?"*

*My cheeks heat slightly. Thank goodness it's dark in here. "Not really."*

*"You're awfully quiet."*

*"I know. I am nervous, but you don't make me nervous. Not in a bad way, anyway." I know I'm rambling, so I take a breath. "I was just stuck in my own thoughts. Sorry."*

*"Don't apologize. What were you thinking about?"*

*"Oh," I pause. I'm not going to tell him I was thinking*

*about sex. "Just happy you're finally back."*

*I force a smile, but when he looks at me, he doesn't return it. Instead he looks very serious.*

*"Do you want to know where I've been?"*

*This may be the last chance I get to find out where he's been. He asked me before, and I left it up to him. He may not offer me another chance to know if I don't take it now.*

*"Yes," I answer softly. Nervously.*

*He sighs.*

*"I was in jail."*

# CHAPTER 11

I PICK UP MY PHONE after the first ring. "Hello?"

"Chevelley, It's Johnny."

"Hey, Johnny. Where you calling from? Your name didn't come up on the caller ID."

"That's why I'm calling. I'm at the hospital."

My heart drops. No, no, no. I can't lose anybody else.

"Why are you there? What's wrong?" My voice is filled with panic.

"Calm down. Everybody is fine. Lou and I were leaving a meeting with Mario and the Muccino brothers—Isaac and Bobby—when we got in a car accident."

"Car accident? Was it really an accident?" I ask, already knowing the answer.

"Someone drove us off the road. We hit the barricade on the highway. We're not hurt too bad. A little bruised up, but we'll survive. They wanted us to come get checked out just to be safe. I'm using a payphone out front since my phone's still in the car. I just wanted to give you a heads up, so you know to be watching your back when you're driving. Roman has many cars, so we don't know what to look for exactly, but be careful."

"Okay. Thanks, Johnny. I'm just glad you're both safe."

"We're tough old bastards. Anyway, I wanted to let

you know that we do have a date set up for Mario to meet up with Roman."

"You don't think whoever drove you guys off the road saw you with Mario, do you?"

"Nah." He sounds confident. "We left first with strict instructions that Mario not leave for another ten minutes, and then the Muccino brothers leave ten minutes after that. Plus, nobody knows Mario is in town yet. He's only spoken to Roman on the phone so far. As far as Rome knows, he won't be in town until tomorrow."

"Okay then. So, what's the plan?"

"The day after tomorrow. Roman has chosen his secluded garage to meet at. It's one of his old chop shops, however, I wouldn't be surprised if he changes it at the last minute, so be prepared for that."

"Alright. Time?"

"9pm."

"If he keeps it at this location, how are we all supposed to get out there undetected?"

"Might be the reason he chose it. You may have to get dropped off out there really early and find somewhere to hide and wait. Roman might have a handful of guys with him, and we'll have to be sure to take them out. The only good thing about this location, is that when the explosive goes off, and with all the gunfire, nobody else will be around to see or hear."

"Well, guess we just hope for the best."

"Yep. I gotta go, though. We'll stop by later tonight or tomorrow to go over everything one more time with everybody."

"Sounds good .Take it easy, Johnny."

"Yep."

And with that, he's gone.

I look over at the clock. Four forty-five in the afternoon. An hour and fifteen minutes from the time I'm supposed to meet up with Xavier.

I spent all last night debating with myself on what was best to do. Something's telling me I should see him, because he has something important to say. I doubt he'd go through this just to warn me off again. Then again, I don't know Xavier like I thought I did. He's different. He lost his heart and soul a few years back. I should know to expect the unexpected from him, because I never expected him to go into business with Roman Rios. Not after what Roman did.

"C?" Gage's voice calls out from the other side of my door.

"Yeah."

The door opens slowly. This is the first time he's approached me since the whole finding out I went to Xavier's house debacle.

"I just wanted to talk to you for a sec."

"Sure," I say, scooting over on the bed to make room for him.

"I'm sorry for yelling at you and being kind of a dick, but you have to understand why."

I nod. "I do. I was dumb. I acted on emotion, and I know not to do that. I was just so devastated and felt so guilty for it all, and all that turned into red hot anger."

"I understand that. We've all been there, but you can't leave the house in the middle of the night and venture into enemy territory. You could've gotten killed. I'd never forgive myself if anything happened to you. I promised your father I'd always protect you. You make it tough to do sometimes," he says with a smile, "but, I love you like a sister. You *are* my sister, and I can't lose you."

"I love you, Gage," I say as I lean in and give him a hug. "I'm sorry. I'm so grateful to have you in my life."

He squeezes me in his arms and then kisses my

forehead. "Good. Let's keep that life going, huh?"

I playfully punch him in the arm. "Fine."

We end up talking about my conversation with Johnny, and we try to come up with a fool-proof plan to get our people out there and unseen. This has to go off without a hitch. If we don't end up killing Roman, we're only gonna piss him off and then who the fuck knows what's gonna happen.

"I wonder if I can get somebody out there to scout the place. That way we know what we're working with," Gage says. "If the meeting will take place inside, I want to know what's all visible from there. Will Roman be able to see his car being tampered with and his driver and bodyguards being taken out? You know?"

"Yeah, let's call up Chase and Ryan. They can go out there, and nobody would connect them to us. Maybe they can get some pictures for us to look at. I doubt Roman will be there, but he might have people watching, so they still need to be careful."

He nods and goes off to make the calls. Chase and Ryan are a couple of guys we're friends with that help us out on small things when need be.

With Gage gone, and after the conversation we had, I've made the decision to not go meet Xavier. I can't risk it. I can't risk my own life.

But, when six o'clock rolls around, I can't help but wonder what Xavier's thinking. Is he pissed? Surprised I didn't show? It doesn't take long for me to find out.

At six-fifteen my phone dings with a text message. It's from an unknown number, but I know exactly who it is.

*We have a meeting. Where are you?*

I don't respond. Five minutes goes by before the next message from Xavier comes in.

> *I'm not a patient man, Chevelley. You're forcing my hand, and you don't want that. By the way, where's your buddy, Gage?*

My blood turns to ice. Does he have Gage? I've been in my room for the last hour, and I assumed Gage was downstairs. I swiftly jump off the bed and fly down the stairs.

"Gage! Gage!"

"Whoa, where's the fire?" Silas asks from the couch.

"Where's Gage? Is he here?" I question in a panic.

"What's wrong with you? No, he's not here. He left a little while ago."

"Alone? Is he alone? Where did he go?"

"C, what the fuck? Why are you panicking? He's with Deacon. They just went to grab some food and beer."

I run upstairs and grab my phone from the bed. I call Gage, but he doesn't answer. I send him a text telling him to call me as soon as he can. I send the same text to Deacon.

The ice in my blood soon turns to fire. I respond to Xavier's text.

> *Where the fuck is he, asshole? I swear to God, if you have done anything to him I'll kill you in the most torturous way possible.*

His response is immediate.

> *Don't make me laugh, Chevelley. You can't kill me. We both know this, don't we? Anyway, you know where to meet me. You have fifteen minutes.*

Now I don't even have a second thought. Thankfully, I'm already dressed in jeans and a T-shirt, so I push my feet into some combat boots that were lying next to the bed. I grab my phone, gun, and keys and ignore Silas' yells as I run out the front door.

Almost fifteen minutes later, I'm pulling up to the rec center. My black Impala screeches to a stop, and my headlights rest on Xavier as he leans against the fence surrounding the basketball court. He looks casual and calm as he checks his watch.

In seconds, I'm approaching him fast and angry. "Where the fuck is he?" I roar.

He shrugs. "I don't know."

"What do you mean you don't know? Where the fuck is Gage and Deacon? What did you do?"

His brows furrow. "I didn't do anything to them."

"Then why haven't they responded to my texts and phone calls?"

Again, he responds calmly. "How would I know?"

"Why did you ask where he was?"

"I saw him. I just figured if you thought I had done something, you'd come running. And look. I was right." He gives me a smug smile.

"You're an asshole."

He doesn't reply to my insult, he only takes out a cigarette and lights it up.

"Many memories here. You remember them?" he asks without looking at me. Instead he begins walking alongside the fence. "We would always park here and," he looks back at me and grins, "well, you know. And the times when we would get out of the car, we'd go over to the field out there with a blanket to look at the stars and just talk. You'd always fall asleep with your head on my chest."

I huff, not wanting to talk about those days. "Is this why you wanted me to come out here? To reminisce? If you don't have Gage, then I'm leaving."

"I never thought that the girl who would fall asleep

in my arms would one day try to kill me while I slept. I was alerted to someone being around my house, and then I saw my gun was missing from my nightstand. I didn't think for one second that it was you lurking in the shadows of my room. Funny how things change, huh? How people change."

That stops me in my tracks. I turn back around to look at him, but he's got his back to me. All I see is the smoke filtering up towards the sky, and him, dressed in dark jeans and a black shirt.

"You of all people should know how easy and fast it is for someone to change," I retort. "I never thought the man who would stay in and watch chick flicks with me while I was sick would end up murdering my friends. Yeah, it's funny alright," I spit.

He turns and faces me. "Chevelley, I warned you to stay away from me. Did I not? I said you'd get yourself killed, and what have you done so far? You've shown up where I'm known to be. My house and Roman's house. I'd think you have a death wish."

"I'm not dead yet. Guess you don't have the balls to kill me."

He chuckles. "I'm not the only one to worry about. You've been spotted. People know who you are and they know how to get to you. You just keep making it easy for everybody, because you seem to go to them. Kind of like you did tonight."

The way he says that makes me look around. Does he have people waiting in the shadows?

"Chevelley, I have to say I'm disappointed in you. You haven't been making smart decisions, and let's not forget that you tried to murder me. That hurts my heart."

"Don't kid yourself. You don't have a heart."

He smirks at me. "Maybe you're right, but if I don't

have a heart, it's only because I gave it away a long time ago." He waves his hand through the air in dismissal. "In any case, you need to know that it's in your best interest that I stay alive. Okay? Because if I die, you die and your friends die."

"What are you talking about?"

He looks behind me and I snap my head around to look as well, but I don't see anything. I look back at him, but now he's looking me straight in the eyes.

"There's a lot you don't know, Chevelley. Things you should never know, but these things are a risk to a lot of people."

I furrow my brows at him. "You're talking a whole lot and not actually saying anything. You killed my friends, Xavier! My family! These guys are my family, and you're taking them away. I have to protect the rest of them, and that's exactly what I'm going to do. If you're caught in the crosshairs, so be it, but I won't risk the lives of my family. You chose to be on that side, and I still don't understand why, but that was your decision. What did Roman say to you to convince you to work with him? How can you even stand to be close to that monster?"

His eyes narrow and his jaw clenches. "You have no fucking idea what I'm capable of! Don't question my decisions, Chevelley, because you could never sacrifice what I've sacrificed! You've led a pretty perfect life considering the life you live. If I told you the things I know, the things that keep me up at night, and the things I'm still doing in order to . . ." he pauses and shakes his head. "You know what? Forget it."

"Perfect life? My father is dead, Xavier! You know how your father died, but I don't know what happened to mine! We never found his body, and had to have a funeral without one! How do you think that makes me feel? To not truly know what happened to him? My life is far from perfect, and I know you've been dealt a shitty hand, too, but we're now on opposing teams. You lost us as your friends and family the day you chose Roman over us. I hope you know how to survive without him, if you survive at all."

Without giving him time to respond, I turn on my heel and head to my car. A large hand pulls me back by my elbow. My right fist instantly flies to his face, but he catches it with his other hand.

"Whatever you're planning on doing. Don't," Xavier growls. "You cannot kill Roman, I won't let that happen."

"Then you can die first. Get the fuck off me," I snarl, ripping my hand and arm away from him.

"Why don't you kill me now? You keep fucking saying it, but you haven't done it yet. Kill me, Chevelley, if that's what you really want."

He stands there with his hands at his side and waits.

Truth be told, something in me is preventing me from shooting him. I know grief-induced anger led me to his house with the intention of taking his life, but who knows if I would've even shot him had he not woken up with gun in hand? Maybe I would've left. Because, if I'm being honest with myself, there's a stupid, small part of my heart that still cares about Xavier.

I turn my back on him and head to my car.

"Don't go through with whatever you're planning, Chevelley. If you do this, it's going to start an even bigger mess than we're already in. You have to trust me."

His voice follows me, but he doesn't.

Once I'm inside the car, all I want to do is scream in frustration. Xavier dropped so much on me, and I now I need to process it all. He hints at giving his heart to me, but then doesn't deny killing my friends, doesn't apologize. Not that I thought he would. He wants to protect Roman of all people! He wants me to not go through with my plan, knowing that if Roman doesn't die, all of us will. What keeps him up at night, and what is he still doing and for what? He never finished his sentence. The man is a fucking nightmare! A beautiful fucking nightmare.

I slam my hands on the steering wheel and rest my head on the top of it for a minute. I can't call off this meeting. We've gone through so much to get to this point. We have people coming in to help us, and we know this has to happen. What bigger mess could be started if Roman is dead?

When I lift my head from the wheel, I look around and notice Xavier is gone. I reverse out of the parking space and leave the parking lot, all while trying to figure out what Xavier was trying to say. It isn't until a couple minutes later that I notice a car is following me. There are a few other cars driving by, but in this residential area there aren't too many. This car, though, is following at a steady pace. I'm going a little under the speed limit since I'm so focused on other things, and this car refuses to pass me.

I make a turn and sure enough the car behind me turns as well. Johnny's warning comes back to me. Did Xavier have someone else there? Is he having me followed?

When I speed up, the other car speeds up. When I turn, they turn. What the fuck? When I finally get to my street, I think about passing my house, but as I slow down in front of the gate, the car passes me and continues to drive.

Am I going crazy?

# CHAPTER 12

WHEN I WALK INTO THE house, I see Silas on the couch with some girl. Her hair is bleached blonde with the ends a bright purple. She's facing him, running her hands through his hair while he watches TV. She's clearly wanting more of his attention, but he's a man, and some football game is on.

"Hey, C," Silas greets with a nod of his head. "Gage is upstairs. He said his phone was on silent when you tried getting in touch, but he and Deacon are okay."

I only nod, because I know Xavier was fucking with me the whole time, anyway. The girl glances in my direction and looks me up and down with a look of disgust on her face.

"Who's she?" she asks Silas in an accusatory tone.

"She is the woman who lives here and owns this house," I answer, walking up to the couch and standing in front of her. "Any more questions?"

This girl better choose her words and facial expressions carefully, because I'm definitely not in the mood for any jealous bullshit.

Once again, she scrutinizes me and then looks at Silas for some sort of confirmation. Silas doesn't say anything.

"You didn't tell me you lived with a girl," she

complains.

"I didn't need to," he replies.

I can tell this girl doesn't mean anything to Silas. He probably invited her over to get laid, and she's just hanging around.

I move to the chair on the other side of the table and sit down. The girl tries to lean into Silas even more and whisper something about him and me being in a relationship. I assume she's questioning if anything has happened between us.

"What?" Silas asks, obviously stunned by her question. "Fuck no, she's family to me," he says, looking pissed off that she even asked.

He shakes his head, and I can tell he's annoyed by her. She seems to be the clingy, annoying type. I decide to help him out.

"Hey, Si. I took care of that Mindy problem for you," I say, pulling my gun from the back of my pants and laying it on the table.

Mindy was a girl he messed around with before and ending up being a complete psychopath. I never actually did anything to her, she eventually moved on, but I figure it's a nice way to scare this girl away.

Silas looks up at me with a small grin and shakes his head. He knows what I'm doing.

"Oh, thanks," he says, before looking back at the TV with a straight face.

The girl's eyes go wide as she looks at the gun then back at me. I smile at her.

"I think I'm gonna go," she stammers.

"Oh? Why so soon?" I ask in a sweet voice.

She looks at Silas who only glances up at her for half a second. "Okay."

Once she scampers out of the house, Silas and I begin laughing.

"You're terrible, you know that?"

"You didn't stop me," I reply. "I could tell she was getting on your nerves. She doesn't even seem your type."

He shrugs. "She came onto me earlier when Gage and I were out. I took her number knowing she was a sure thing."

I just shake my head. "I'm gonna head to my room. I'll see ya later."

"Okay. Oh, wait. Why did you seem so scared earlier? About Gage."

"I thought he left alone, and he wasn't answering my calls, and I'm sure you can imagine what I thought happened."

I rush upstairs before he can ask where I ran off to, because I don't have an answer for him, and telling him about Xavier doesn't seem like a good idea. I already don't know what to think about what X said. Even if I told the guys we couldn't go through with our plan, I'm sure they'd do it anyway, because it would be dumb not to.

Tomorrow we'll get photos from Ryan and Chase and finalize our plan to get up there, hide, and execute Roman and everybody that comes with him. Then this fucking war will be over, and we can go back to focusing on our clients.

I strip out of my clothes and make my way to the master suite and turn the shower on hot. Once the bathroom is filled with steam, I step into the shower and adjust the temperature to something that won't scald my skin.

In the shower, where it's quiet and void of distractions, I do my best thinking. I go over everything that needs to be done, and come up with plans on how to complete them. I think about how my father would be handling things, and hope that he's proud of the job I'm doing.

I know I'm not perfect, and I still make mistakes from time to time, but I'll learn from them. That's a true leader; someone who can admit to failing and use those failures to succeed.

Xavier's words come back to me and I once again try to decipher what he was saying. He was so conflicting. I never for a second thought he gave his heart to me. We never exchanged I love yous, even though I yearned to say it. I wasn't a hundred percent sure he'd feel the same way, so I kept it to myself.

I never had the time to build up enough courage to tell him how I felt. It was like one day everything was fine and we were happy, and then things suddenly went south.

People had started realizing we were a little more than friends, but everybody seemed to like Xavier. My dad knew we were all friends, but since Xavier and I didn't define our relationship, I never felt the need to tell my dad that he meant something to me. My dad didn't dislike Xavier, but I bet if he knew we were fucking, he would have made sure to keep him far away from me. He probably assumed Gage would do that for him, but Xavier used to be a good guy, a guy we all thought we could trust and like, so Gage didn't mind that I spent a lot of my time with Xavier.

One day tragedy struck, and Xavier was never the same. None of us were. It was a domino effect of bad happenings.

With a sigh, I finish up my shower and then crawl into bed. I turn the TV on and flip through channels until I land on something that catches my attention. Porn. Terrible soft porn, but porn nonetheless. Based on the title alone—The Virgin Housekeeper—I assume our porn star plays the innocent virgin. The man seems to be a busy CEO, and of course sparks fly between them. When they finally get to the first sex scene, I laugh out loud. For a virgin she sure does seem to be enjoying getting rammed from behind. Maybe he has a small dick.

I'm reminded of my first time. Xavier definitely doesn't have a small dick, and we definitely didn't do any other position besides missionary that first time. Xavier was considerate and romantic. A far cry from what he is now.

***Past***

*"You were in jail?" I ask.*

*He sighs again. "Maybe we can make something to eat at my house and talk there. This isn't really a conversation I want to have in public," he replies.*

*"Okay."*

*We stay silent the rest of the way to the house. The only noise is the soft music drifting through his car speakers.*

*When we pull up to his house, he comes around and opens the door for me. I take his hand as he leads me up the concrete path to his front door. The house looks like a nice starter home for a family. Two stories, a small yard, and the tiniest of front porches. It looks to be an older house, but it's not in bad shape.*

*He flips the light on when we get inside and while it's obviously a guy's house, it's not as messy and plain as you'd expect. Xavier doesn't bother showing me around, instead we go straight for the kitchen.*

*"I'm not sure what you want to eat. I wasn't expecting to make anything, really," he says as he looks through the freezer.*

*"Xavier," I say softly. He takes a breath before turning to look at me. "We don't have to make anything. Just come sit and talk to me."*

*Truthfully, I couldn't eat much right now even if I tried.*

*With the nerves of what tonight holds, and now the mystery of why he was in jail, I'd probably end up pushing food around my plate more than putting it in my stomach.*

*He closes the freezer and takes a few steps to reach me as I stand near a counter at the entrance of the kitchen. Taking my hand in his, he leads me past a stairway and small dining area, and into his living room. The couch we sit on has two oversized, brown cushions. It's surprisingly really soft and I fall back into the removable back cushions instantly.*

*"When I told you to wait for me," he begins, "I had a feeling something might happen. I was set to meet up with someone who was wanting to buy guns from my father. My dad told me to be careful, because he didn't trust the guy. The man who was buying the guns wanted me to carry one with me to prove we had the kind he wanted.*

*"I don't normally carry them on me, because if I'm ever caught I could get arrested for illegal possession of a firearm. This man was insistent, and my father needed the transaction to go through, so I agreed. I was set to meet him the day after I saw you at the club. I had the gun with me, but he wasn't at the meeting location, and coincidentally, a police officer was. He saw the gun, and that was that."*

*"Illegal possession of a firearm usually has a longer jail sentence than six months," I reply.*

*He gives me a small, amused grin. "You're right. However, I knew if I ran, dropped the gun somewhere and was caught, it would be harder for him to prove I had the gun on me at all. So, that's what I did. I was caught, and the gun was found, but without fingerprints. After a while, and with some pressure from some friends my dad has in his pocket, the charges had to be dropped, and I was released."*

*"Lucky you," I say with a smirk. "What happened to the guy who was supposed to buy the guns?"*

*His face hardens. "Nothing. He claimed it was all accidental. He was running late, and the cop just happened to be in the meeting place. Why he decided to search me was also questionable, but I won't get into that. Without actual proof, my father decided to continue to do business with him."*

*"Who is he?"*

*"Roman Rios."*

*"Huh," I reply. "I'm pretty sure I've heard my dad talk about him."*

*"Yeah, well, tell him to watch his back, because Roman can't be trusted."*

*I nod. "Well, I'm glad you're out and back in town."*

*"Yeah?" he questions with a grin. "How happy?"*

*He scoots closer to me, his brown eyes boring deeply into my own dark eyes. My breathing instantly speeds up and my gaze goes to his mouth. His lips are perfectly proportional, framed by his mustache and goatee, with a scruffy beard beginning to line his jaw.*

*"Really happy," I breathe, bracing myself for his next move.*

*"I'm really happy you're here with me, Chevelley," he says. The way his accent twirls around my name makes me weak. His voice is like honey. Thick, rich, and smooth.*

*He grabs me by the waist and pulls me onto his lap in a straddling position. Xavier doesn't speak any words as he removes my blazer and pushes my black hair over my shoulders. His eyes rest on my D cup breasts as his hands trace my curvy waist and land on my ass. He pushes me forward, causing me to grind on him and releasing a groan from both of us.*

*"I know you said you waited for me, but does that mean I still get to own your innocence?" he asks, meeting my gaze once again.*

*I nod because I'm unable to find words.*

*Without hesitation, he stands up, and I wrap my legs firmly around his waist while he walks upstairs. He plants small kisses on my neck and chest as we make our way to his room. Once inside, he places me gently on his bed.*

*"Don't be nervous," he whispers. "I'm going to take my time with you."*

*He then moves down my body and takes my heels off, dropping them onto the floor. His hands rub my legs as he moves them upwards, ending with his fingers dipping into the waistline of my leggings and slowly peeling them off of me.*

*A chill runs up my spine at the same time warmth forms in between my legs. Xavier straddles me, and starts pulling off my tank top. I sit up enough to help him get it and my bra off.*

*Naked, I lie back down on the cool covers, thankful there aren't any lights on; only the glow from the street lamps and the moon shining through the window. I begin feeling a little uncomfortable, being on full display, but Xavier soon eases my comfort.*

*"God, you're exquisite," he says, his voice a low rumble.*

*In a quick motion, he rips his shirt off and throws it to the floor. I gape at his beautifully sculpted torso. While Xavier isn't a really bulky guy, he's definitely got muscle, and his ripped abs are like a work of art. It looks like he's constantly flexing when that certainly couldn't be possible. His arms are tanned and toned to perfection; his biceps the perfect size. He has a small happy trail leading to what I'm sure will be my happy place, and a very small smattering of hair on the middle of his chest.*

*He chucks his jeans next and is left wearing black boxer-briefs. I don't get much time to enjoy the view of his body, because he's soon hovering over mine. My hands wrap around him and hold onto his back.*

*Very slowly he leans in and kisses my lips, and then he starts a trail of kisses across my cheek, down my neck, and across my chest. I try not to pant loudly as he moves his mouth down to my right nipple. His large hand grabs the meaty flesh of my breast and he sucks my hardened bud into his mouth. My back arches and I let out a moan that fills the room.*

*Xavier moves to the other breast and shows it the same attention before planting kisses on my stomach, moving at a slow pace down to the apex of my thighs. My breath comes in heavy pants now, and I can do nothing to stop it.*

*I watch his head move in between my legs, and with one last glance into my eyes, he begins licking the length of me. A loud gasp rushes out of me as I grip the covers tightly in my hands.*

*"Oh, God!" I moan.*

*I look down and see his tongue snake out and lick me again, parting my lips, and tasting my wetness. He makes love to my pussy with his mouth, and it's the most unbelievable feeling I've ever experienced. His licks and kisses are soft, yet intense.*

*His tongue begins probing my entrance and my eyes squeeze shut as my back once again arches off the bed. I've masturbated before, and even used some small toys, but nothing compares to Xavier's mouth, tongue, and lips. I fear I might burst into a million pieces once I find out what his dick can do.*

*"I'm going to slide my fingers inside of you now, okay?" he says in a husky tone.*

*I look down at him and nod frantically. One finger slides in, and then another finger. His tongue flicks my clit at the same time, and I feel like I might die. The sensation is overwhelming. I reach down and grip his hair in one hand while he slowly brings me to the brink of explosion.*

*I scream out as my orgasm takes over my entire body.*

*Xavier kisses and caresses what seems like every inch of my body before finding my mouth and giving me a deeply passionate kiss. His hand moves to the back of my neck, and his tongue dances flawlessly with my own.*

*When we break apart, he climbs off of me and makes his way to the nightstand. He pulls out a condom, placing it on the table while he removes his boxer-briefs.*

*His erection is long and thick; the veins protruding*

*through the tight skin on his shaft. The sight of it both excites and frightens me. I hope my eyes aren't as wide as they feel as I wonder how the hell he's going to fit inside of me without ripping me apart.*

*Grabbing the foil packet from the table, he slowly makes his way back onto the bed and between my legs.*

*"It's going to hurt for a little bit, but trust that I'll do everything I can to make this the most enjoyable experience of your life," he says while ripping open the package.*

*I nod as I admire the magnificent man in front of me. His naked body, sculpted to perfection in every way, causes my body to ache for him. I've already had one orgasm, but he's quickly making me desire another one while I watch him grab his hard length and sheath it in latex.*

*He spreads my legs apart and situates his body before me, his dick touching my pussy momentarily causes me to tense up.*

*"Relax, Chevelley," he says, soothing me.*

*I try to relax my body as much as possible, and then I feel his engorged head prod at my entrance. He inches his way in so very slowly and cautiously. I almost wish he'd give me one quick thrust to get it over with, but I appreciate his consideration.*

*A burning sensation hits me and I squeeze my eyes closed tight as I cry out. Xavier then fills me up completely and holds still. The burning and pain is still present, but Xavier hovers over me and kisses me deeply and fervently, and I decide to focus on only that. He soon begins moving inside of me, and my nails dig deeply into his skin, but he doesn't show any sign of pain.*

*While slowly thrusting inside of me, he kisses my neck, sucks on my nipples, and caresses my body. Everything he does not only takes my mind off the pain, but it gives me pleasure which makes my pussy wet, and allows his thickness to slide in and out easier.*

*Xavier worships my body in a way I didn't know possible. I know I have nothing to compare this experience to, but there's no way anybody can do it like Xavier does.*

*He gives me another breathtaking orgasm, and soon enjoys his own orgasm. The sound of his deep voice bellowing through the room sends chills throughout my body. The fact that being with me causes him to make such blissful noises amazes me.*

*I fall asleep in Xavier's arms for the first time, hoping I'd never have to know what it was like to not have him in my life.*

# CHAPTER 13

A PHONE CALL FROM JOHNNY wakes me up. He informs me that he, Lou, Chase, and Ryan are on their way over. I quickly get dressed, settling for a pair of jean shorts and a white T-shirt. I make sure Gage and Silas are up before calling Rem, Deacon, and Trax, and telling them to head over.

I make a pot of coffee, and while I'm pouring myself a cup, I hear a quick rap on the front door before Rem's voice calls out.

"Hello?"

"In the kitchen," I reply.

All the guys have the code to the gate, so they're able to let themselves in, which is why it's never a surprise to hear the front door open without having let anybody in.

"Ooh, coffee. Make me a cup?" he asks as he enters the kitchen.

"Make yourself a cup," I reply, hopping onto the counter.

"I love your bitchy side," he says with a grin.

I laugh. "My only side."

"Nah, you have a sweet side, too."

I roll my eyes and take a sip. "You come alone?"

"Yep."

"Goddammit, Rem! You know you aren't supposed

to be out alone. Where's Deacon and Trax?"

"They take too fucking long to get ready. They're like women. I went by their place, and they were just getting up, so I left."

Deacon and Trax are roommates. Rem lives on the same street, but prefers to live on his own.

"You drive me insane, you know that?"

"You mean drive you wild, right?" he says with a wink.

I ignore him and take another sip of coffee. After Rem makes his coffee, he leans on the counter across from me and takes a sip. He's wearing a white T-shirt that has a black skull design, but the sleeves stretching around his biceps is what catches my attention. If he flexes even a little bit, I wouldn't be surprised to hear the material tear. His blue eyes are bright, and his blonde hair is combed back, with the sides looking to have been cut short recently.

"Maybe you should stop working out, Rem. Looks like you're gonna rip through that shirt any minute now."

Gage walks in. "Nah, he just needs to stop shopping at baby gap."

Gage and I both laugh as Rem looks down at himself.

"This is a fucking double X. Fuck you guys."

"Whatever you say, man," Gage responds as he looks for a coffee cup.

The guys always rip on each other, so nobody takes any real offense. They're all used to it.

I hop off the counter and make my way to the living room while Gage and Rem start talking about some shit I don't care about. Silas sits next to me right as Trax and Deacon walk in.

"Are Ryan and Chase here yet?" Deacon asks.

"Nope. They'll be here soon," I answer.

Deacon wears a black shirt, black jeans, and a black baseball cap. He pulls off the hat to run his hand through his thick, brown hair, before dropping it back on his head. He has in his hoop nose ring, which I think only he can pull off.

"Hey, Deac. Hear from Lee lately?"

He shakes his head at me as he drops into the chair. "Nah. She's playing hard to get."

"She probably don't want you to catch her," Trax jokes.

"Oh, she wants to be caught alright, she just wants me to work for it."

"Hey, C," Trax says, walking behind me and touching the top of my head.

"Hey. There's coffee in the kitchen, but Rem and Gage are in there talking about cars, I think."

"I'm good," he responds, before coming to sit on the other side of me.

Trax hates talking to Gage and Rem about cars. Those two can go on and on for hours about what cars have what engines and all kinds of other shit I have no knowledge of. I don't blame him for hating those conversations.

The four of us watch TV until the other guys show up a few minutes later. We all settle around the large dining room table as photos of Roman Rios' garage are spilled in front of us.

"Okay, here's what we got," Lou starts. "Chase and Ryan were able to get up there when nobody was around and get some photos for us. This right here," he says, pointing to one photo before passing it around, "is where the main entrance is. You might not be able to tell from that photo, but it's not facing the road that you drive in on. There's two large windows on either side of the actual garage, but again, nothing faces the road."

He passes around a few pictures for everybody to look at. It's definitely secluded with no other buildings or businesses around. However, it doesn't give us much room to hide.

"Where are we supposed to be waiting?" I ask.

"Well," Johnny chimes in, "there's a work shed that sits about twenty feet from the main building. Three people can fit in there. There's also an old truck that's sitting on the lot, and it doesn't seem to be getting worked on. It's risky, but we can have a couple people waiting in the bed or the cab of the truck. We don't expect more than a handful of guys to show up with Roman."

"The good thing about the truck is the access it gives you to whatever car Roman shows up in. I have no doubt that they'll pull right up close to the door. You can expect Roman to wait inside the office of the building until Mario shows up," Ryan says. "The truck isn't too far from where he should be parked, and it'll be easy for your guys to hop out, and do what they need to do to his car."

"What if he waits in the garage portion?" Gage asks.

"That would be better, because the garage is further away from the car and faces the opposite direction. All you gotta hope for is that they don't park directly in front of the garage."

"And if they do?" Deacon asks.

Silence settles over everyone.

"Then there's going to be a whole lot of bullets flying," I say. "We cannot let Roman leave the garage alive. So, by any means necessary, we have to take him out."

"Ryan and I can take you guys out there well before Roman is expected to show. It'll give you time to scope out the place before getting to your hideout spots."

All of us spend some more time around the table, going over the pictures and a few possible scenarios depending on what happens out there. It's dangerous, but having Roman stay alive is even more dangerous.

I can't help but think about what Xavier said last night, but there's no way I'm telling the guys we can't do this. Roman's death can't possibly cause any more of a mess than his life would.

"Alright. Everybody be here tomorrow by six-thirty," I announce. "I want to make sure we have plenty of time to drive out there and get settled. The only thing we have working for us is that it's going to be dark. Be sure to wear dark clothing, and bring every gun you can."

A few of the guys linger in the dining room to talk while I go outside and light a cigarette. This whole fucking war shit has caused me to start smoking even more than I used to. I told myself I was going to quit, but then this shit happened, and I knew there was no way I would be able to go without my cigs.

I take a few long drags before Silas joins me.

"So, where'd you go last night?" he asks.

Fuck.

"What?"

"Last night. When you ran out of the house like a crazy woman? Where did you go?"

I take a drag and glance at Silas from the corner of my eye. He's staring me down, and I know he's not gonna let this go.

"Nowhere," I answer with a shrug.

"Don't bullshit me, C. You know I know better."

I huff. "You're really fucking with my cigarette break."

"Chevelley," he growls.

"I went and saw Xavier, okay? I thought he had taken Gage, so I went to him."

Silas lets out another low growl. "You could have not come back, you know that, right?"

"Yeah, well, I'm back. Xavier obviously didn't have Gage, so I came back home."

"Why hasn't he fucking killed you yet?"

"Excuse me?" I screech.

"You know what I fucking mean. You keep going to him. He comes here, you go to his place, and now you go to wherever the fuck you went to meet him, and yet you're still alive."

I don't say anything. All I do is take another drag and look to the sky, because I've thought the same thing, too. I've seen Xavier kill someone before. It was a few years ago, and he didn't know I was there. It was actually a man who was causing problems for one of our clients, but I guess he was causing problems for Roman, too. Xavier killed him before we had the chance to deal with him.

I've seen the cold, callous look in his eyes before taking a life. If you look into his eyes, you see a man with nothing left to lose. He has no fear and no worries, and that's scariest of all. So, why has he not killed me? I'm sure Roman wants him to.

"And also," Silas says, breaking into my thoughts, "why is he still alive?"

I snap my head in his direction with a scowl on my face, but all he does is raise his eyebrows at me. I understand his question, but don't want to start that conversation.

"Silas," I say on a sigh.

"Look, I know you probably have feelings for the guy. I liked him, too. Not like you did," he says with a laugh, "but, he was a good guy before. He's just not the same anymore. I need you to be careful around him. You know he can flip like that," he says, snapping his fingers.

"I know."

I throw the cigarette to the ground and stomp on it before going back inside and trudging upstairs to my room. Within a few seconds I have Lee on the phone.

"What's going on, C?" she answers.

"Not much." After a pause, I rethink my statement. "Actually, that's a lie. A lot is going on."

"Roman and Xavier stuff?"

"Yeah."

"You wanna talk about it?"

I sigh heavily. "Tomorrow we're set to take out Roman, but I spoke to Xavier and he basically warned me off of that idea. He said he wouldn't allow that to happen, but also said it's in my best interest to keep him alive. I don't know. It's such a fucking mess."

"So, Xavier told you he needs to stay alive, and apparently Roman as well?"

"Yeah, but that doesn't make any fucking sense. He said if we were to try to kill Roman, it would make things messier. I don't see how. It's only a problem, because Roman is still alive. Roman not being around anymore fixes everything."

"You know it's hard to trust Xavier. He's been working with Roman for a while now. They're probably pretty close. I don't know how that's possible, considering, but in some fucked up way, they're friends."

"I don't get it either. He also hinted around things he's sacrificing, and things that keep him up at night. He also mentioned that he gave his heart away. I don't know if he was just fucking with my head or what."

Levi gasps. "He was talking about you? Giving his heart to you?"

"I thought so, but we never talked about our feelings or anything. He's probably just fucking with me."

"I don't know. I always thought he cared about you a lot more than he let on."

"Whatever. Everything is just stressing me out. I'm worried about the outcome of tomorrow. I can't lose anybody else."

"Well, I can't lose you, so you better be careful."

"I know," I say quietly.

"Wanna talk about something else?" she asks.

"Yes, please."

Lee and I continue to talk on the phone for an hour or so. Our topics range from Deacon, to her brother pissing her off for showing up to her house drunk, and her parents annoying her with wanting family dinners every Sunday. I remind her how it's good that she has parents—parents that want to spend time with their children at that.

It feels good to talk to Lee and free my mind of the cluster fuck that is my life right now. At least for a little bit.

When we hang up, I take a quick shower and then end up back downstairs looking for food.

"Lookin' sexy, C," Trax calls out after a whistle.

I roll my eyes. "Fuck you."

I'm wearing plaid, faded pajama bottoms, and a large sweatshirt with a couple holes in it. I know he's being a sarcastic asshole.

He laughs as I make my way to the kitchen. After looking through the fridge and freezer, I decide it might be nice for all of us to have a nice dinner together tonight.

"Hey! You guys eat?" I yell.

"Nah. You cooking?" I hear Gage ask.

"Yeah."

I pull out the pork chops that I had defrosting, and begin making smothered pork chops and rice for my guys. My family.

Once everything is done, Gage helps me take

everything to the dining room table, and we all sit down to eat. I'm at the head of the table, with Gage sitting at the other end. Rem sits to my right, Silas to my left, and Deacon and Trax fill the other spots. Lou, Johnny, Ryan, and Chase already went home.

We all look at each other, living in this moment; branding it to our brains, because even though it's not spoken aloud, we know this could be the last time all of us are at this table.

"I want you all to know how much I love all of you. I appreciate everything you've ever done for me, for each other, and for my father and his business. I couldn't imagine not having you in my life and in my corner. You all have sacrificed so much for this job, and I'll never be able to repay you. Just know that I appreciate you," I say, looking directly in each of their eyes.

"You've done plenty for all of us, C," Rem says. "We'd do anything for you, because we know you do everything with us in mind."

"There's no need to thank us, Chevelley," Silas says. "We're family, and having each other's backs is what we do. No questions asked."

I smile, trying to hold back the tears that threaten to fall. With a nod, I begin to eat and everybody follows suit. We laugh and reminisce about the past. We talk about Jai and Jasper, making sure to keep their memory alive. Everybody jokes about something stupid one of us has done, and we talk about my father. He was a father to everybody at the table. He was loved dearly, and now he's missed deeply.

After dinner, we don't bother putting the TV on, we only continue to talk and enjoy each other's company. It's not until midnight that we disperse. Trax, Rem, and Deacon all go home, while the rest of us go to our rooms in the hopes of getting plenty of rest.

I'm not sure about the guys, but it takes me a long time to actually fall asleep. Different scenarios for tomorrow run through my head. I think of the worst possible outcomes, and the best ones. I try to prepare for anything, but know I'll never be fully prepared.

I'm not sure what time my mind finally shuts down and allows me to sleep, but when I do, I'm tortured with memories from the past. Memories that haunt me in my dreams, making sure I never forget some of the best and worst moments in my life. Both of which I'd love to erase from my mind.

# CHAPTER 14

***Past***

*"COME ON, CHEVELLEY. IT WON'T be that bad. I'll be with you the whole time," Xavier pleads.*

*"Do you want to be with me while I throw up all over the place? Because that's what's gonna happen. I don't know why you guys are forcing me to do this," I complain.*

*Me, Gage and his girl Jackie, Silas, and Xavier all traveled to Six Flags Great Adventure in New Jersey. They're now in the process of getting me to ride the Batman rollercoaster. Now, I've tried some of these other rollercoasters, just trying to be a good sport, but this one? Fuck this one.*

*"Come on, C!" Gage pleads. "We're all going. We want you to be with us."*

*"Please, babe," Xavier begs with a faux pout.*

*Xavier and I have been "dating" for a year now. We've never had the relationship talk, but we spend as much time together as possible. We don't have the boyfriend-girlfriend label, but we don't see anybody else. I think we both just know that we're together exclusively without having to ask "What is this?"*

*Gage and Silas are friends with him, so it makes it easy for us all to be together. My dad doesn't know the extent of our relationship, which is probably a good thing, but he's also a parent, and they seem to know things even when you think you're being slick and getting by on them.*

*I love Xavier. I fell hard and fast. He's told me he cares about me, that he'll always be there for me, and protect me, but he hasn't said the L word, so that makes me nervous to bring it up. There would be nothing more embarrassing and painful than putting yourself out there and expressing your feelings, leaving you raw and open, just to have some salt poured on you when your significant other doesn't respond the way you want them to. So, I enjoy what we have now, because we're happy and that's all that matters.*

*"Fine, but if I throw up, I'm aiming for all of you!"*

*Everybody laughs, and as we walk up to the long line, Xavier grabs my hand and brings it to his mouth. His lips lay a few soft kisses to the back of my hand, and his eyes stare deep into mine. He gives me his lopsided grin that melts my heart, and it's times like this that I don't need him to say he loves me, because I can feel it. And feeling somebody's love for you is so much better than just having the words said to you.*

*I return his smile and lean in to give him a kiss.*

*"Better kiss me now before I have puke breath."*

*A deep, low chuckle passes his lips. "You won't puke, babe. I have faith in you."*

*He's right. I don't puke. Jackie does. Thankfully, she doesn't throw up until after we get off, though.*

*"Ugh. I'm not riding that one ever again," I say, rubbing my head. "I still feel fucking dizzy. I don't like all that spinning shit."*

*"Wanna go on the Big Wheel? It's high, but it's slow." He looks behind us at Silas, Gage, and Jackie. "Plus, we can be alone," he whispers, waggling his brows.*

*"Sounds like a plan!" I chirp. "Hey, guys! Me and X are gonna go on the Big Wheel. We'll meet up with you after."*

*We rush off to get to the one hundred and fifty feet high Ferris wheel, and wait in line for about twenty minutes before being allowed on.*

*Once inside, Xavier puts his arm around me and pulls me in close. I rest my head on his shoulder and revel in his warm embrace. The sun is starting to go down, so they've put the lights on. The ginormous wheel is lit up with colorful, bright lights, creating a floral design that enhances the experience. It's now more romantic with amazing views of the park and beyond.*

*"How's business going?" I ask.*

*"My father seems to be having some trouble."*

*"Oh yeah? What's going on?"*

*"Roman," he growls. "He's pushing for some weapons, but my father doesn't have them. The shipment that was coming in got seized, so we have to wait. Roman doesn't seem to understand or care. He's pressuring my father to get them from somewhere else, but we don't like to venture away from the guys we trust."*

*"Understandable. My father got a call the other day. I heard him talking about guns, which I found odd since we don't really deal with that."*

*"Hmm."*

*"I didn't question what was going on, because my father seemed pretty pissed. He doesn't seem to like Roman too much."*

*"I'm not sure many people do."*

*"I haven't met him."*

*"You don't want to." He pauses for a while. "Are you learning a lot from Memphis? I heard you go along with the crew now."*

*"Yeah, he's pretty much taught me everything. I hang around him when he's conducting the business side of everything, and when it's time to handle an enemy of a client, I've been able to go. Well, most times. There were times when he thought it best I stay behind."*

*"Why's that?"*

*"Mob bosses. He doesn't want me being seen by them just yet."*

*"You aren't scared of this life, Chevelley? Murder, violence, and everything else?"*

*"X, you know I've been around it my whole life. I don't know a life without these guys and this lifestyle. This is the norm for me. I've witnessed the violence, but I understand why it's necessary. I've witnessed murder, but I knew that it was them or us. Come on, you've probably witnessed more than me. Are you scared?"*

*"I have been."*

*His answer shocks me. "When? Why?"*

*"I'm not afraid for me. I feel confident I can protect myself. I'm afraid of losing people I care about. People close to me." He stops speaking for a good minute. "I'm afraid of losing my father, and I'm afraid of losing you. I don't think much about relationships, but if I ever thought I'd get a girl, I never thought she'd be involved in the same shit I am. So, not only do I have to watch my back, I have to watch yours, too."*

*"You don't have to watch mine. I got it covered, and I have plenty of other guys who are willing to protect me as well."*

*He grins at me. "I'll always watch your back, no matter how many other people vow to protect you, and no matter how confident you believe yourself to be. I know without a shadow of a doubt, that I'll be the one to keep you safe. I wouldn't be able to live with myself if I let anything happen to you. So, while I know you can handle yourself, I will always be there to watch your six."*

*I roll my eyes. "Watch my six? Really? Why not just say watch my back?"*

*He shrugs. "I like six better."*

*"I appreciate that. I do." I think for a minute. "Did you call me your girl?" I ask with a smile.*

*He chuckles and squeezes me into him. "I'm glad I have you, Chevelley. Even though you're in the same lifestyle, and it worries the hell out of me, you understand my life and don't judge it. I couldn't ask for more."*

*I feel his lips plant a kiss on my temple, and I snuggle in closer.*

*"I love today," I say.*

*"Me too, C. Me too."*

*ON OUR WAY HOME, XAVIER gets a call. His voice sounds like a mixture of anger and nervousness. I sit in the backseat with him, watching his jaw tense and his fists ball up. He doesn't say much on his end, so I'm unsure of who may be on the other side of the call and what they're saying. I just know it's not good.*

*When he hangs up, I don't ask right away what's going on. He seems on edge and extremely pissed off. So pissed off that he's completely silent. I wait, knowing I should give him time, and he'll say what he wants to when he can.*

*After five minutes, I rest my hand on his thigh. His large hand covers mine, but he doesn't look at me. I'm already missing his beautiful smile and warm eyes.*

*His voice is barely above a whisper when he speaks, but the tone is stern. "Roman paid my father a visit."*

*I gasp, my hand flying to my mouth. I've heard of Roman's work, and I can't imagine what he might have done to Xavier's father, nor do I want to. I wait in silence. The other passengers sit quietly up front in the truck. Jackie seems to be asleep on Gage's shoulder while Silas drives.*

*"Things are going to get bad, Chevelley," he says in an ominous tone.*

*"What's happening?"*

*He doesn't answer. I can tell by his rigid posture and inability to look me in my face that he's still angry. Understandably so. He's working out a plan in his head. He's dealing with his emotions in the best possible way under the circumstances; in a car full of people.*

*Silas looks at me through the rearview mirror. His face reflects how I feel. Worried.*

*The rest of the ride home is awkward and uncomfortable. Nobody says a whole lot of anything, so I just pretend to fall asleep.*

*We all know the dangers that lurk in the shadows, and the monsters that hide in broad daylight. We're well aware of the constant threats of violence against people we know; the grim reality that we will lose someone close to us eventually, but we still hope for the best. Because, once all hope is gone, all we have is a never ending sea of despair.*

*All I can do now is hope Xavier's father is okay, hope that he'll continue to be okay, and hope beyond hope that Xavier is able to handle whatever happens to his father. The Roman I've heard about doesn't leave people alive once they've pissed him off, so dread sits heavy on my heart. If X loses his father, I'm afraid of the man he'll become.*

*When we get back to my house, Xavier gives me a chaste kiss before rushing to his car and heading home. I don't allow myself to feel hurt, because I know he has a lot going on, but I wish he'd let me be with him. I offered my support, but he wants to be alone.*

*"Roman hurt his dad?" Silas asks, as we watch X speed off.*

*"Yeah, I'm assuming so."*

*"Over guns?"*

*I shrug, because I really don't know. Gage tells his girl to wait in the house before coming towards me and Silas.*

*"Memphis got a call from Rome the other day."*

*"I know," I say. "What was that about?"*

*"Rome says Memphis can get the guns he needs from one of his clients, but Memphis refuses to ask a client for weapons, especially since we don't deal with that shit."*

*"So, I'm sure that pissed Roman off," I reply, a little worried that my father might have just pissed of the one guy you shouldn't.*

*Gage shrugs. "He didn't say too much."*

*"I don't like this, guys," I say softly.*

*"Let's try not to worry about it until we have to," Silas responds, putting his arm around my shoulder and walking me to the door.*

*For the next two days I don't hear from Xavier and begin getting worried. His phone goes straight to voicemail, and he doesn't reply to any text messages. I finally convince the guys to go with me to his father's place, because I have a feeling that's where he's gonna be.*

*"Maybe he just wants to be alone. Maybe he's taking care of his dad, C. I'm sure he's fine, just a little preoccupied," Gage says.*

*"I'm not being a clingy girlfriend, I just want to make sure he's okay. We don't know what happened to his dad. What if it's really bad and he needs his friend's help and support. What if Roman came back? We gotta make sure he's okay."*

*Neither one of them says anything else. When we pull up to Victor Delgado's house, I instantly spot Xavier's car in the driveway. I feel a hint of relief, but I still feel the need to see him to make sure he's actually okay.*

*All three of us approach the front door, Gage and Silas making sure to check the surroundings while I knock on the thick, wooden door. A minute goes by, and Gage bangs on the wood even louder. After another minute goes by and nobody answers, I try the door handle. To my surprise, it opens.*

*"Xavier?" I call out. "It's me, Gage, and Silas. You here?"*

*Silence answers back.*

*"X, we're gonna come in, man," Gage yells into the seemingly empty house.*

*We make our way into the small foyer, closing the door behind us, and then follow the hall into the living room. A few things are knocked over, and a handful of items are broken; picture frames, beer bottles, and a ceramic figurine Victor had on his table.*

*"This doesn't look good," Silas whispers.*

*Continuing to walk through the house, we don't find any sign of Victor or Xavier. The rooms are empty, the kitchen and bathrooms are empty, which only leaves one place. The basement.*

*"If they're here, they're in the basement," I say quietly. "But, I don't understand why they would be."*

*"Let's check it out," Gage says.*

*We find the stairs at the very back of the house and cautiously tread down them. There's a door that opens into the basement at the foot of the steps, and we find it slightly cracked open. Gage puts his finger to his lips, making sure we stay quiet.*

*When he moves over, I peek into the room and spot Xavier and Victor. I gasp, but Silas is quick to cover my mouth, because it's not only Xavier and Victor in the basement. Roman and three other men are in there.*

*I realize that none of us brought our guns with us. It was a stupid decision, but one we really didn't think to make, because we never thought we'd need them just coming to Victor's house.*

*Xavier is on his knees and has duct tape over his mouth with his hands tied in front of him with rope. His father is nearby in the same position.*

*Roman's voice bellows throughout the basement.*

*"You thought I would allow you to fuck me over on this deal and get away with it?" He laughs a very humorless and cold laugh. "Don't you know me better than that by now? I will always get what I want, and if I don't get it due to someone's gross incompetence, they will pay for it."*

*Roman has a strange look about him. I feel like he was once handsome, but has gotten into one too many fights. His nose looks like it's been broken a handful of times, and the scar under his eye is visible from where I stand; about ten feet away. His hair is a little long, and the spattering of black and white facial hair shows his age.*

*He has a face that is pure evil. It lacks emotion, and I'm almost positive he'd kill his own mother if it got him ahead in life.*

*Victor tries pleading with him, but his voice is muffled due to the tape.*

*"You need to learn to make better friends, Victor. One of your associates had the wherewithal to help you, but chose not to. It's partly because of him that we're in this predicament. Mostly your own fault, though, let's not kid ourselves.*

*"Maybe your son would do a better job than you. Perhaps I should start doing my business strictly with him, because he doesn't seem to have a problem following through with things. I respect him. He went to jail because he brought a gun I asked for. Now, unfortunately, I wasn't able to meet him that day," he says, running a hand over the front of his crisp shirt. "But he didn't rat me out to the cops as the person looking to buy."*

*Roman looks over at Xavier who, if looks could kill, would be viciously killing Roman right now. His forehead is wrinkled, his brows furrowed, and eyes intense. He loathes this man.*

*"Then again, maybe he's useless just like you, just like your friend Memphis. Maybe I should rid the world of all of you."*

*My heart drops to the pit of my stomach and bile burns my throat. My father. He's threatening my father.*

*Victor tries talking again, but Roman ignores him, deciding to pace in front of them instead while his men stand behind him.*

*"I gave you a chance, Victor, and that was only because I haven't had problems with you before. I've enjoyed our business relationship, but you've now failed to deliver to me twice,*

*and that's too many times. I can't allow others to think I'm going soft. But, I will give you a choice." He pauses for dramatic effect. "Who dies?"*

*He steps towards Victor and rips the tape from his mouth.*

*"Please don't, Roman. The shipment is coming. It should be here tonight. You don't have to kill anybody."*

*Roman shakes his head slowly. "Tsk tsk tsk. That's not the answer I was looking for. Maybe I'll choose." He points his gun to Xavier's head.*

*On instinct my body jolts forward, but the guys hold me back. They know we don't stand a chance right now.*

*"No! No! Please don't."*

*"Memphis then? He could have helped. Shall I kill him and that sexy piece of ass he calls his daughter?"*

*It's then that Xavier makes a noise and starts fighting against his restraints.*

*"No, not them either," Victor says sadly. "Just kill me, but promise me you won't hurt my son."*

*Xavier struggles some more, making inaudible noises while staring at his father. Tears trickle down my cheeks.*

*"I won't kill him," Roman states, staring at X. "No, I won't kill him."*

*The tone in his voice is strange, like he's somehow fascinated by Xavier. In a half a second, his gun is trained on Victor's head and the trigger is pulled. He has a silencer on, but my body still jumps at the sound.*

*My stomach lurches at the sight of Victor's blood splattered on the wall behind him, small rivers of red dripping to the ground. Xavier groans into the tape and tries to move his body closer to his father. I can't control my sobs, so I rush upstairs before I'm heard.*

*I run out of the house, and Gage and Silas soon follow. They force me into the car and speed away.*

*"We have to do something," I cry. "We have to call the cops!"*

*The guys are quiet for a few seconds, probably taking in the scene they just witnessed.*

*"We can't call the cops, C," Silas says, sounding remorseful. "If the cops show up to that house, Xavier goes to jail. That house is full of weapons that would put him away for a long time."*

*"Do you think we could have stopped them?" I ask, tears dripping off my chin.*

*Gage sighs. "We would have been killed. We don't have weapons and each of them had their weapons in hand."*

*Deep down I know he's right, but I feel terrible not being able to do anything. To watch Xavier watch his father die in front of him. Should I tell him? Would he be upset that we didn't help? Would he understand? Then there's the situation of my dad. Roman seems to put blame on him for what happened to Victor. I can't help but wonder if Xavier feels the same way, and will in turn come to hate me and my father.*

*I curl into myself and sob even louder. My heart feels like it exploded when that gun went off, and I can only imagine what Xavier is feeling right now.*

*"Let's grab our guns and head back. If Roman is still there we can avenge Victor's life."*

*"Our place is too far away," Gage replies. "We're stopping by my friend's place. He lives a few blocks away."*

*I feel a smidge better that we're at least going to try to do something. Plus, we need to get back to free Xavier and make sure they really didn't kill him.*

*After Gage runs into his friend's house, he exits with a bag in hand, and I can only assume it holds weapons. He tosses the bag to me before climbing in and speeding off in the direction in which we came.*

*I unzip the black duffle bag and begin pulling out the handguns his friend supplied us. I make sure each one is loaded and ready to go.*

*Before I know it, we're only a few houses from Victor's.*

*"How are we gonna know if they're here still? They obviously didn't park out front before, or we would've noticed an extra car."*

*"It doesn't matter if they're in there or not. We go in thinking they are," Gage answers.*

*When Gage pulls up along the curb at the house next door, I hand them their guns, and we hurriedly get out and run up to Victor's front porch. Gage opens the door with a quick shove and instantly has his gun trained in front of him. When he recognizes nobody is there, he jerks his head, letting us know to follow him.*

*Silas and I follow him inside, our guns aimed and ready as well. We make sure to clear each room we walk through as we make our way to the stairs that lead to the basement. With each step my heartrate picks up, making my already shattered heart feel like it might beat out of my chest and land at my feet in a bloody heap.*

*The door leading to the basement is open wider than it was before, leading me to believe the men who were in there have already left. Gage, taking no chances, makes sure to peek inside, gun ready to shoot in a half a second if necessary.*

*I move in behind him, my eyes focused on the lifeless body of Victor Delgado lying on the floor. My eyes squeeze shut, and I try to force the tears from falling again. I can't fall apart right now.*

*"Where's X?" I whisper, noticing he's not where he was when we left.*

*"Don't know," Silas whispers back.*

*The basement seems to be empty of people, which would be a good thing if I knew where Xavier was.*

*While Silas and Gage make sure to check the dark corners and behind boxes that are stacked three or four high, I go to the other side where I know a bathroom to be. I need to grab some tissue and get myself together.*

*I push open the door and find the light switch. When the*

*fluorescent light flickers on, my breath catches in my throat.*

*"Xavier," I whisper.*

*He sits on the closed toilet, his head in his bloodied hands. His head slowly comes up and when he looks at me, I can see a change in him already. While his eyes are noticeably red, they also look vacant. The Xavier I was with a couple days ago no longer exists.*

*Xavier doesn't say anything to me. He doesn't really react at all. All he does is drop his head back in his hands.*

*"Are you hurt?" I ask cautiously.*

*He shrugs in response.*

*"We saw, Xavier. We saw everything. I'm so sorry." I drop to my knees in front of him and leave my gun on the floor. "We came to check on you and saw Roman down here. We didn't have our guns, X, or we would have tried to prevent it. I'm so sorry," I weep. "We left and went straight to Gage's friend's place, got some weapons and came back."*

*"It doesn't matter," he says in a clipped tone.*

*"We can get revenge, Xavier. We can make sure Roman pays for what he did."*

*His head jolts up, blood covering his temples and forehead from his hands. I assume he touched his father after he was freed. Just imagining that scene makes the tears burn behind my eyelids.*

*"Roman will not pay for anything," he says through gritted teeth. "You cannot lay a hand on Roman, do you understand me?"*

*My brows furrow in confusion. "What do you mean? He has to pay! Why don't you want to see revenged exacted?"*

*He shakes his head. "I can't explain this to you right now."*

*Xavier stands swiftly, stepping past me like I'm not even here. Gage and Silas walk up to the door as X washes his hands in the sink.*

*"Fuck. You okay, man?" Gage asks. "I mean, are you hurt?" he says, changing the wording of his question, because*

*of course he isn't okay.*

*"I'm not hurt," Xavier replies in more clipped words.*

*"We can help you with your father," Silas offers, knowing we'd have to come up with a plan regarding his father's death. We can't call the cops here, but he needs a funeral. We'll have to plant his body somewhere else and pretend we don't know what happened. The cops will find out what it is Victor was involved in and how he made a living, which means they won't investigate too much into his death. Revenge killing, gun deal gone bad, mob hit, perhaps even a drug deal gone wrong. They don't give a shit about us "street criminals," so they don't bother wasting money on an investigation, which in this case works out for us.*

*"I got it," Xavier responds.*

*"You sure?" Gage asks.*

*"Yeah. I got help already."*

*The three of us exchange looks, but don't say anything.*

*"Did Roman say anything to you?" Silas asks. "Do we need to worry about him doing anything?"*

*"He said plenty," Xavier snarls. "You don't have to worry about me."*

*I almost hear an emphasis on the word me, but I'm not sure.*

*"We'll make sure he gets what's coming to him," Gage growls. "He's a fucking thorn in everybody's side. Especially lately."*

*Xavier spins around and looks Gage and Silas in the eye. He then makes sure to look over at me before speaking. "I'm only going to say this once. You will not lay a finger on Roman. Leave it alone."*

*Xavier's tone is dark, threatening, and unlike anything I've heard from him before, at least to us, his friends.*

*"Leave it alone?" Gage asks, baffled.*

*"Leave it the fuck alone," Xavier replies before pushing through the two men and leaving the bathroom.*

*"What the fuck?" Silas mouths.*

*I shrug, because I have no earthly idea why he wouldn't want Roman to die.*

*All three of us follow Xavier out of the bathroom, and when we find him, he's shoving his phone in his pocket.*

*"I appreciate you all coming, but I'm gonna need you to leave now. I gotta take care of my father, and I'd just rather be alone right now."*

*Confusion, hurt, and sadness fill my body and mind. I don't understand Xavier's behavior. I don't know why he doesn't want our help, or why he seems to care so much about Roman all of a sudden. I want to be with him, comfort him, and help him through this, but he seems set on being alone. I try not to take it too seriously. He did just lose his father, and I might want to be alone, too, if I was in his situation. But, something definitely seems off. I just can't put my finger on it.*

*"Okay," I say slowly. "Call me when you're feeling up to it, and let us know if you need anything."*

*"For real, man. Anything," Silas says.*

*Xavier nods once at the guys. I walk up to him and give him a small kiss on his cheek. He turns his back, dismissing us, so we all trek back up the stairs and out of the house.*

*When we pile into the car and drive away, we notice a dark blue van pulling up to Victor's house. We're out of sight before anybody gets out.*

*"What the hell?" Silas asks, voicing all of our thoughts.*

*"I don't know, man. Shit was weird in there. I think he's struggling with what happened. I don't believe he wants Roman to stay alive. That's just fucking insane. Let's give him some time," Gage states.*

*We drive home in a daze.*

*I instantly go to my room as soon as I'm home, and fall to my bed and cry. I cry for Victor, I cry for Xavier, and I cry for myself. I still see the blood and brain matter flying all over and sticking to the wall. I see the blood dripping into a pool on the concrete below Victor's body. I see Xavier's cold, dead eyes. I see the serious and threatening look on his face as he tells us to leave Roman alone.*

*Assuming we'll be invited to his father's funeral, I think I'll at least hear from him within a week or so.*

*The call never comes.*

*Days go by.*

*Weeks go by.*

*I call Xavier numerous times until one day an operator says the phone has been disconnected.*

*When I do see Xavier again, he's nothing like the man I thought I loved.*

*He confuses me.*

*He scares me.*

*He makes me not want to see him ever again.*

# CHAPTER 15

THE SUN COMES UP AND goes down unusually fast today. Before we know it, it's six-thirty, and we're all gathered in my living room, getting ready to drive to Roman's garage.

With every weapon we could possibly use, Gage, Silas, Trax, Rem, and I are driven up to the empty lot. After determining that nobody else is here, we hop out of Chase's suburban, and begin looking around. The Muccino brothers followed behind us in Ryan's car, and Deacon is parked further away, allowing him to see who comes and goes. If anything goes wrong, he'll be able to follow someone as they leave, or if everything goes as planned, he'll come pick us up when everything is over with.

We try to open the door to the building, but it seems even though this place is out of use, Roman makes sure to keep everything locked up. Gage finds the tool shed, and if you keep the door cracked marginally, you have a good view of the garage.

I spot the truck and take a peek inside the bed, finding a tattered blanket and blue tarp riddled with holes thrown inside. Could be used for cover, I suppose.

After we get a lay of the land, we gather near the suburban.

"I think I'm gonna lay in the bed of the truck. One of you can be with me while three of you can wait in the tool shed." I look at the Muccino brothers. "You guys can be in the cab of the truck. Hopefully they park nearby."

"I'll stay with you," Rem offers.

"Okay. Chase, what time do you have?"

He looks in his car. "Eight."

"We have an hour until Mario is supposed to meet up with Roman. Since we don't know how early Roman might show up, I think we should get Chase and Ryan out of here and be in our places."

Gage nods and we all say good-bye to Chase and Ryan who wish us luck. I send a text to Deacon to let him know what's going on, and then we all make sure our phones are on silent.

Silas pulls me into a quick hug and kisses the top of my head. "Be careful."

"You too," I reply into his chest.

Gage gives me a single nod and squeezes my hand in his. "We'll see each other when this is all done."

I nod, a lump forming in my throat, thinking *I hope so.*

Isaac and Bobby crawl into the front seat, making sure to stay low as Rem and I climb into the back of the beat up truck and pull the blanket and tarp over us as much as possible. We leave our heads uncovered for now; the rank smell of the material almost makes me gag.

"You doing okay?" Rem asks.

"Yeah. Honestly, I can't wait for it to be over."

"I gotcha. Things need to go back to normal."

"You don't think this, us doing this to Roman, will cause any other problems, do you?"

"No. Why?" he asks, seemingly confused as to why I'd think that.

"I don't know. Just curious."

The real reason? Xavier. I wish I knew what he was getting at, but when it comes to Roman, he's always been so strange.

"We gotta do this, C. You know that."

"Yeah. I know."

A few minutes later, I feel two quick vibrations from my phone. I maneuver my body and pull the phone from my back pocket. One text is from Deacon saying cars are on their way. Another text is from Lou letting me know Mario got the call and is on his way up here.

I pass both messages along to everyone else with instructions not to text back. Roman will be pulling up within minutes.

Soon, the sound of tires on gravel fill the quiet air around us. We pull the covers over our heads, but are sure to have our guns in hand. I try not to focus on the moldy smell of the blanket, and instead listen to the noises around us.

One car door closes, and then another. They aren't too far away, I'm guessing parked behind the truck, which means they'll have to walk past us. One more door closes before we hear voices. I can make out at least three different ones.

Footsteps near us, causing my adrenaline to pump along with the rapid fire beats of my heart. A small tear in the blanket near my eye allows me an obscured view into the night. I see a couple heads pass by, not paying any attention to the truck, and I silently breathe a sigh of relief.

Keys jingle.

Someone coughs.

A couple more footsteps.

It sucks being blind to what's going on. I want to know what they're doing.

"Son of a bitch." The voice sounds like Roman's. "It's

too fucking dark. PJ, I think I have a flashlight in that truck over there. Go get it. I can't fucking see which key I need."

Shit. Shit. Shit.

Not the fucking truck. I squeeze my eyes shut briefly, pissed that this isn't going to go the way it needs to. All because of a stupid fucking flashlight.

My gun rests on my stomach, my hand gripping it tightly, ready to shoot as soon as the blanket gets ripped from me. PJ's footsteps get closer, and I hold my breath. Rem is motionless next to me, and I hate that we can't communicate to come up with a plan.

"Where at, boss?" PJ's voice booms. "The front or the back?"

"Just fucking look!"

The keys jingle some more, and then I smell whatever cologne PJ must have put on today. He's close. Too fucking close.

I hear a pop followed by a creak.

"Never mind. I got it."

PJ's footsteps move away and I let out the air I was holding in my lungs.

"What's wrong, Xavier?" Roman's voice asks. "What're you looking at?"

Fuck. Xavier is with him.

"Nothing. I just thought I saw something."

I wish I knew what direction he was looking in. Did he see movement by the tool shed?

"Nobody would be out here," Roman replies with confidence.

Think again, mother fucker.

The door to the building closes and after several minutes of absolute silence, I'm sure all three of them are inside.

"That was fucking close," Rem whispers.

"I know. Too close."

About five minutes later, the door creaks open again, and the scent of cigarette smoke hits my nostrils. It's a damn better smell than this moldy, dusty blanket, but I don't like that someone is standing nearby, leisurely smoking a cigarette.

I hear the sound of footsteps move further away, and then soon after, they're back again. Whoever it is seems to be scoping the place out. I mentally cross my fingers and hope they don't look in the tool shed. The steps seem to move away again before walking alongside the side of the truck. He—whoever he is—hits the side of the truck as he walks by causing me to tense up. I fear he's climbing back here or opening the bed to get something, but seconds go by and nothing happens.

"Everything good?" Roman's voice asks after I hear the door open again.

"I think so," Xavier responds. "You sure this is the best spot to meet him at? Perhaps we should have met him at the warehouse."

"Do you think this place isn't secure enough?" Roman questions, his voice partly curious, but also somewhat offended.

"I'm sure it's fine," Xavier answers coolly.

It's silent for a few moments before Roman speaks up again. "Well, Mario wants to see some of the weapons I have available, and I keep those particular ones here. So, here is where we'll meet."

Xavier doesn't bother responding.

"Looks like he's here," Roman says.

A minute later, the sound of a vehicle approaching fills the silence.

"Did he bring anybody with him?" Xavier asks.

"I'm sure he has one person with him. He'd be a stupid fuck to come alone." He pauses. "I'll be in the garage. Bring him and whoever he's with in there. And, where the fuck is PJ?"

"Last I saw him he was inside."

"Get his fucking lazy ass out here, too. He needs to know how to handle something like this."

No more words are spoken, and several seconds later, I hear the sound of the garage being opened. One car door closes after the other, and their footsteps approach the truck.

"Mario," Xavier greets. "Roman wants you and your guest to come with me."

"Alright," is Mario's calm response.

I can only assume Xavier escorted Mario and whoever he brought to the garage, and then came back, because the door squeals as he pulls it open.

"PJ," he shouts. "Get your ass out here."

"What's goin' on?" PJ asks.

"Roman wants you in the garage."

I wait a couple minutes until I'm sure they're all in the garage looking at weapons before I make a move. We won't have much time, so we can't waste what we have. I poke my head over the side of the truck and don't see anybody in sight. I knock on the back window of the truck lightly until Isaac's head pops into view. I motion for him and Bobby to get out and do their job.

They sneak out of the front seat, making sure not to close the door all the way behind them, and go to the black Lincoln that's parked about ten feet behind the truck. I spot the car Mario must have come in. It's a charcoal gray SUV of some sort, and he made sure to park it along the side of the building, giving him distance from Roman's car.

Isaac and Bobby begin working on Roman's car as soon as they reach it. I spot their bag on the ground, carrying everything they need to make this work. Earlier,

I heard them discussing how they wanted to activate it. Apparently, it's going to be triggered by depressing the accelerator, which is the best option, because it won't be until they are driving away that it'll go off.

They had said it wouldn't take too long, but we don't know how long this meeting is going to last, and they can't be caught outside, they just can't be.

I hear the sound of deep-voiced laughter bellowing through the air from the garage. Whatever they're doing or talking about seems to be going well.

I take another peek over the side of the truck and check on Bobby and Isaac only to see them starting to make their way to the truck. I give them a thumbs up in a way of asking if everything went okay. Bobby nods while Isaac gives me the OK symbol.

Thank fucking God. Now, as soon as they get in the car, all we have to do is wait for everybody to leave. We could possibly get through this night without firing our weapons and risking lives.

My relief is short-lived as I hear voices and footsteps making their way around the corner. Bobby and Isaac aren't in the truck yet, and won't be able to get in without being seen. I flatten my body in the bed right after I see Bobby and Isaac drop to the ground. Their only choices are to lay under the bed and hope to not be seen, or stay crouched down on the side and hope nobody walks around and spots them.

My breathing starts to get heavier as panic tries to take over my body. Rem is stock still and I'm almost worried he fell asleep. As if he knew what I was thinking, he reaches over and squeezes my hand. I feel a little calmer knowing he's ready and by my side if anything happens.

"So, you're happy, yes?" Roman asks.

"Oh, yes. Very happy," Mario responds. "Very

impressed."

"Great!" Roman exclaims with a loud clap. "We can finish discussing everything in my office. PJ, take this key and lock up the garage. I'm gonna take it off the ring, because I need the keys to my office and drawers. Don't fucking lose it."

I hear keys clanking together.

"Shit. Sorry, boss," PJ stammers.

"What the fuck? I just told you don't lose it and the first fucking thing you do is drop it. What the hell is wrong with you?"

"I'm sorry. I'll find it."

"You're goddamn right you will or you'll be staying out here all night until you do. Get the flashlight from the truck. You won't be able to see through all these rocks and dirt."

"Yes, sir."

"Jesus Christ," Roman mumbles.

The door opens at the same time PJ's footsteps approach the truck. This is it. He's going to start feeling around in here, looking for a flashlight, but finding us instead. Once I shoot him, the guys will come running out of the building, and my guys will run out of the shed, and then all hell will break loose.

I hear him cursing Roman under his breath right before his hand starts pushing around old cans that sit in the corner near my head. The blanket moves slightly, uncovering part of my head, and I know it's only a matter of time before he spots me.

His hand touches my hair. "What the fuck?" he whispers.

The blanket is ripped off of me and his eyes widen in shock. I don't give him time to yell out or pull his own weapon. Mine has been ready in my hand, so all I do is lift, aim, shoot.

The bang echoes throughout the night air, and he drops backwards onto the ground with a bullet hole in his head. It was either him or me, and I'll be damned if I let it be me.

I don't have time to think about what just happened, because angry voices begin running towards us. Rem is already up and out of the truck, and I'm quick to follow.

Isaac and Bobby follow us as we run around the side and out of sight before Roman and Xavier exit the building.

I tell the Muccino brothers to get into Mario's SUV and stay low. There's no need for them to get mixed up in this. They're only here because we asked for their help.

Hiding on the side of the building, I peek my head around the corner and see Roman, Mario, Mario's partner, and Xavier staring down at PJ's body.

"What in the fuck?" Roman roars.

Xavier looks annoyed. I feel like he already knows I'm here, and he's pissed I didn't listen to him. Mario looks a little worried, and I don't blame him. He wasn't allowed to carry any weapons. It's one of Roman's demands when doing business, however Roman still carries, and it's proven when he pulls a gun from the inside of his jacket and aims it at Mario.

"You do this? Huh? You have something to do with this you lying fuck?"

Rem moves around me so swiftly, I don't even have time to figure out what's going on until I see that he's approaching Roman from behind. I have no choice but to follow him.

The door to the tool shed opens slowly and I see the guys trickle out.

Xavier turns back and spots Rem first. Rem pulls the trigger at the same time Xavier pulls his gun from his pants and fires in our direction.

Roman yells out, obviously hit, but so is Rem. I see his left hand go to his shoulder, but he keeps his gun aimed at Xavier.

Suddenly, Roman whirls around, clearly hearing my guys approach him from the other side. He fires off two shots, but more shots are fired back at him.

He ducks, bringing his arms to cover his head, and runs for the old truck we were just hiding in. I watch as he climbs inside and am surprised to hear the old thing start up.

"Rem, we have to stop him."

My heart is racing faster than it ever has. I feel like my entire body is tingling with electricity. I'm not scared. I don't have time to be frightened. I'm pissed and I'm focused. Roman cannot get away. He's seen us now. This will definitely turn into that larger mess Xavier was talking about if he gets away.

Gage and Silas are firing shots into the truck while Rem and I try shooting the tires.

Bullets whiz by my head and over my shoulder. The continuous loud shots penetrate my eardrums. I quickly glance to my right and see Xavier, but now he's firing at Gage and Silas, trying to prevent them from hitting Roman.

I direct my attention back to Roman and the truck, but my heart plummets as I see that he's getting away. Turning to aim at Xavier, I'm shocked to see he's no longer there.

"Where's X?" I shout, running towards the building.

"Don't know," Gage answers.

"Where's Trax?" Silas asks.

"Fuck!"

We all run towards the building, Gage and Silas choosing to go inside, while I go running around the right side.

"Rem, you alright?" I ask, jogging towards him.

"I'll be alright," he answers, "It wasn't too bad."

"Good. Text Deacon. Let him know to be on the lookout for Roman."

He nods, pulls his phone out and heads around the left side of the building.

As I'm rounding the back corner, I hear Gage shout out, "Found him! He's been shot."

I turn around, wanting to get to Deacon as soon as possible, because I don't know how grave he is. But, as soon as I take my first step, an arm comes around and hits my wrist, causing me to drop my gun. A hand covers my mouth firmly while the other arm wraps tightly around my chest, trapping my left arm between my body and his.

I try to bite the flesh of the palm, but because of how hard he's pushing his hand into my face, I'm unable to. I kick behind me a few times, landing two of the three, but not seeming to do any damage.

"Stop fighting, or I will kill every one of your friends who's here with you tonight."

Xavier.

With my only free arm, I fight back as much as possible. I punch, elbow, pinch, and scratch. I try to find his eyes with my fingers, but he's able to dodge my hand. Xavier's strong, and he has my body pinned so tightly to his, my movements are limited.

Disobeying him may not be the smartest thing to do, but I refuse to go down without a fight. If I fight him, it could slow down whatever plan he has, and maybe the guys will find me. He'll kill me before he kills them, and I'd rather that than anything.

"I said to fucking stop," he growls, clutching me even tighter to his body. "You're coming with me. I'm going to remove my hand from your mouth, but you better not scream. I mean it, Chevelley. Shut the fuck up, and just do what I say."

As soon as he removes his hand, I open my mouth to scream. I get out *Ga*—the beginning of Gage's name—before I'm hit over the head with brute force. My world goes black.

# CHAPTER 16

I WAKE UP SLOWLY, AND with a throbbing pain in my right temple. Lifting my hand to touch the aching flesh, I flinch and quickly draw back my hand. There's a lump, and I'm sure an ugly bruise is already forming.

Suddenly, remembering what happened, I panic and begin looking for my gun. It's not in the back of my pants and my extra one is not in my boot. Shit. I wonder if Xavier brought me to Roman. Well, I don't even know if Roman's alive. I certainly hope he's not.

I look around slowly, taking in my surroundings. I'm on a small bed, probably a twin size, in a fairly small and empty room. The only light I'm getting is from either a closet or a bathroom to my left, the door has been left open a few inches.

There are no windows, and that sends shivers down my spine, because it lessens my chance at an escape.

Curious about the room with the light, I get up from the bed and cautiously make my way to the door. When I push it open, the hinges let out a loud screech, causing me to freeze and wait for someone to come barging in. When nobody arrives, I step into what happens to be a bathroom. Well, if you could actually call it that.

There's a toilet with a dark ring in the bowl. The floor is white and yellow linoleum that looks like it was made in the seventies. The pedestal sink looks worse for the wear, fitting in perfectly with this bathroom. There's no mirror, no shower, no towels, and no toilet paper.

When I walk back into the main room, I feel around on the walls, looking for a light switch. I find that the walls are concrete, which makes me think I'm in a basement. That would explain the no windows.

When I do run across a switch and flip it up, nothing happens. Just fucking great. I keep walking the perimeter of the room, looking for the door that would get me out of here. Not that I think I'd really be able to walk out, but it's worth a try.

Like I thought, when I find the door, I also find that I'm locked inside.

There's nothing else in the room besides the bed, so I go back over and sit on the edge. I guess all I can do is wait. But, wait for what? For who?

I don't know how much time goes by, but as I'm leaning against the headboard and rubbing my hands nervously over my jeans, I hear a noise at the door.

Sitting up straight, I brace myself for who I'm about to see and what might happen.

"You're up," Xavier says, acting like I just woke up from a nap instead of being knocked unconscious. "Before you try anything, know that I have a gun, and that even if you were to get past me, you wouldn't get much further."

He closes the door behind him, and I watch his shadowed figure move across the room.

"What do you want, Xavier?" I question.

"I want you to listen to me for once in your life," he says, sounding frustrated. "I told you to not make a scene, and what did you do? Tried to make a scene. Jesus, Chevelley. Something's wrong with you."

"Yeah, I'd say I have bad taste in men," I snarl.

Xavier actually chuckles. Asshole.

"How did you get me here? Where are all my friends?"

"Don't you worry about them."

"I will worry about them!" I yell, sitting up straighter. "You shot Trax and Rem! I can't fucking believe you."

He lets out an annoyed sigh. "If you would've listened to me about not going through with your little bullshit plan, then I wouldn't have had to shoot them. You put me in that place, Chevelley."

"Oh, so it's my fault? I'm to blame for you shooting people? That's rich."

"I told you not to do it. I told you I wouldn't allow you or anyone else to get to Roman. Didn't I? I tried to help you. I told you you'd cause a bigger problem, but of course, you didn't listen."

"Is Roman still alive?"

"Don't worry about Roman."

"What about Trax? Did you kill him? You can at least tell me that."

He shakes his head slightly. "You're so naïve sometimes, Chevelley."

"Fuck you!"

"Ah, there's typical Chevelley."

"You're a bastard! If you're gonna kill me, just get it over with already. I don't want to be held prisoner in this dank fucking room. It's disgusting."

He ignores my outburst and comes to sit on the other end of the bed. I can see his face clearer now. They always said the devil was handsome.

"I'm gonna tell you a story." I open my mouth to protest. "Ah ah," he says, lifting his hand that holds the gun. "You're going to want to hear this story. I promise." He pauses and looks like he's trying to figure out how to start. "Remember the day my father died?" he asks.

That question comes out of left field. If I was expecting anything, it definitely wasn't that. Xavier never spoke to me about his father's death. He was a different man afterwards.

"Yes."

"Well, when you all left, Roman stayed for about ten or fifteen minutes. I was still tied up and unable to talk, but he had plenty of talking to do for the both of us." He takes in a deep breath. "Roman threatened you and your father that day."

"I know. I was there for that."

Xavier shakes his head. "He knew I was angry. Beyond angry. I was furious, and he knew that the moment I got the chance, I'd have a bullet in his head. So, he made sure I wouldn't be able to do that."

I cock my head in confusion. "I don't understand."

"He said he would tell someone to kill you and your father if anything ever happened to him. He knew you and I were messing around back then. I'm not sure how he knew, but that's beside the point. He said if I wanted to protect you, I'd have to protect him."

I gasp, my hand flying to my mouth. My eyes go wide with shock and I just stare, unable to find words.

"I don't know who he told, it may even be a few people, but if he dies at the hands of me or the hands of one of your crew, you're dead."

"Did he kill my father?" I ask, a lump caught in my throat.

"I don't know," he answers softly.

"You better tell me if you know, Xavier! You better fucking tell me the truth!" I yell, a few tears trickling down my cheeks.

"I suspect, but I don't have solid proof."

"Oh my God," I sob.

Xavier stays silent while I try to get myself together.

Now that I know of his threat, I don't doubt he had something to do with my father's death. I try to think back to the time before he died, in the hopes of remembering something going on between them two. My father never liked Roman, and once he found out about Victor, he hated him even more. Roman seemed to have disappeared for a while after he killed Victor, though.

Years later, in the months leading up to my father's apparent murder, he was having problems with somebody. He refused to talk about it, saying it was fine and he'd take care of it, but maybe it was something with Roman. Maybe he was trying to get back at him for killing Victor? For blaming Victor's death on him, even though it was strictly Roman's own doing.

If he pissed Roman off, then perhaps he held true on his promise. For whatever reason, I was left out of it.

"So, all these years working for him was for what? To keep me and my father alive?"

"After he made that threat, he left to go ensure it would be followed through, and his guys stayed behind to untie me. If I would have been untied while he was still there, I would have killed him with my bare hands.

"After you left, he and his people came back to help me with my father. Believe me, I was sick to my stomach the whole fucking time. I wanted to hurt him. I imagined strangling him, putting fifty bullets in his body, anything you could think of. He knew it, too. He laughed and said, 'You want to kill me, don't you, boy?' I just grit my teeth and kept quiet. Roman said he would make sure I had a job and money if I worked for him. My father's business died with him. I hadn't built relationships with all his clients. I was just the middle man, and so without him, I didn't have anything to keep me afloat."

I'm stunned silent, equally enthralled and disgusted

by the story.

"I knew that by working with him, I wouldn't be able to be with you. He wouldn't allow me to interact with any of you, because he didn't trust me. It took years for me to earn his trust. We left town, and he taught me his business. He told me he needed someone like me on his team, and that he hoped I wouldn't let him down.

"I started realizing that not only could I earn his trust, but maybe a few of his men's trust as well. Maybe I could get a few guys to turn on him, and find the person he told to kill you, too."

"So, that's why I couldn't get in touch with you," I say, almost in a whisper. "And, that's why you warned me to not do anything to him. Because if he died, I died."

He nods. "And if I died, he wouldn't have any qualms about finishing you off. As long as you were alive, he knew he had me in his pocket."

"You killed my friends," I state.

Once again, he shakes his head. "Chevelley, it wasn't me who killed Jai or Jasper. Jai died at the hands of the man you killed in the shed. His first shot at you missed, and hit Jasper who was standing behind you."

"But, I saw you go in that shed with some sort of weapon, and when you came out there was blood on it."

He looks at me strangely. "I thought somebody was there earlier that day. That was you?"

"Yes, and I saw you, so why are you lying?"

He huffs. "I'm not lying. I went in there, yes, but I didn't kill him. Jai was dead already. Paul—the man you killed—had already done his business. He had orders from Roman to carry out, and he did. I was handed the weapon and told to go in there and make sure he was actually dead, because Paul said he hadn't actually checked for a pulse. You see, Paul doesn't just shoot someone. He's more torturous and I'll spare you the details, but Roman wanted to make sure he wasn't just unconscious. When I went in there, I placed the hatchet on the already bloodied table. I checked for a pulse, and found he was indeed dead. My anger and frustration got the best of me, so I threw some shit around in there before leaving."

"What about Rem and Trax? You shot at them. I saw that for sure."

"Chevelley, if I wanted someone to be dead, they would be. I shot them where I knew it wouldn't be fatal, but also to where I knew it would slow them down. I couldn't have Rem shooting at Roman. I couldn't allow Trax to try to take me down. And, if Roman noticed that I wasn't doing anything to help him, he'd have my head on a platter."

I drop my head into my hands, shaking it back and forth in disbelief. As soon as I touch my bruised temple, I hiss and pull my hand back.

"I'm sorry about that," Xavier says, gesturing to the injury he caused.

"Are you?"

"Well, again, you didn't listen to me. You were trying to scream when I told you not to. I didn't have time to explain everything to the guys back there if they found me with you. Plus, they probably would have shot me on sight."

"What did you do with Bobby and Isaac? The only vehicle there was the one I told them to hide in."

"I made them get out," he says, matter-of-fact.

"How did you make them get out?" I question, narrowing my eyes at him.

"I didn't hurt anybody, if that's what you're worried about. I might have scared them, but I needed the car."

I inhale deeply and blow it out. "I just can't wrap my head around all of this. You did this for me? For my father? Knowing it would ruin things between us?"

"I didn't want you to experience the pain of losing your father. Unfortunately, you did anyway, but I tried my best to keep that from happening." He hesitates, staring deeply into my eyes. "I also wanted to make sure you were safe, because even if I couldn't be with you, I didn't want to exist in a world that you weren't apart of. You're too important to a lot of people, and you did nothing to deserve Roman's wrath."

I scoff. "I have now."

Xavier's mouth twists up into an almost smile. "But, now you know I'm on your team. I've always been on your team."

Butterflies take up residence in my stomach, and my heart soars. Could this really all be true?

"Remember that night on the Ferris wheel?" he asks.

"Of course I do."

"What did I say to you that night?"

"That'd you'd always watch my back."

He nods. "And that I knew without a shadow of a doubt, that I'd be the one to keep you safe, no matter what."

"Xavier," my voice cracks. "All these years. You gave up so much."

My soaring heart comes back down and splinters in my chest.

"I gave up you. I had nothing else to lose, but I did have hope. Hope that I'd be able to find my way back to you, and that was only possible if you lived. I sacrificed myself, my sanity, and perhaps my moral compass, but it was worth it if you were still alive. Worth it, if one day I'd be able to tell you the truth and you'd understand. Worth it, if I was able to avenge my father's death."

My eyes study his face for what seems like forever, trying to find the right words to say. I'm not sure there are right words for this situation. It's so fucked up.

"Xavier, you let me hate you for so long. You let me believe you were a monster who was capable of killing my friends and threatening my life. You were so good at convincing me of those things that I even went to your house to kill you. Oh my God, I can't believe it. How can you even be here with me?"

"I told you it hurt my heart," he replies with a sad grin. "You just didn't believe me."

"I feel awful and stupid, and just plain embarrassed," I say, covering my face.

He pulls my hands down. "Don't be. If I was truly that person, which you believed I was, then I completely understand why."

"Why didn't you tell me earlier?"

"People follow me wherever I go. I always have someone watching out for me, so if they saw me going to you for a reason Roman didn't know about, suspicions would arise. Plus, I was hoping to have information regarding your father before talking to you about this. I wanted to have already convinced some of Roman's guys to turn against him, choosing to help me take him down, and helping me convince you this whole thing is the truth." He studies my face, a sincere look overcoming his. "Do you believe me, Chevelley?"

I think about it for a moment. "I do." He looks relieved. "You said people follow you. Was somebody there that night we met up at the rec center?"

He nods once. "Yeah, which is why I had my guy follow you, and my guy isn't one of Roman's guys. I wanted to make sure you got home safe."

"The one who came to my place with the note?" He gives me another single nod. "Well, I guess I should say thank you. So, thank you, Xavier, for doing all of this for me."

Xavier gives me a smile. A genuine, beautiful, perfect smile that I haven't seen in so long. Warmth shoots through my veins, filling my body with a heat I haven't been accustomed to as of late. I'm used to seeing his cruel smile, his mocking smile, the smile he put on in an effort to play his role in keeping me alive.

"So, what now?" I ask. "What's going on with Roman? What about my guys? Do I get to tell them what's going on?"

"Well, Roman's alive."

"But, we're gonna kill him, right?" I question, hoping he gives me the answer I want.

"*We* aren't killing anybody. *I* am killing him."

"What about the guys?"

"They need to know the truth now. I won't be able to do what I need to do if they're trying to kill me as well as him. So, tell them what you want, and if they want to talk to me later, we can, but it'll be hard to do under Roman's watch."

"Where does Roman think you are now?"

"He's at the hospital. I'm sure he's not too concerned about much right now."

"So they did hit him?" I ask, feeling good about that.

"Yeah, a few times. Nothing fatal, though."

"What will you tell him happened?"

"The truth for the most part. I was able to shoot a couple of your people before getting away. I'll tell him we'll come up with a plan to finish this, but in the meantime, I'll be talking to some of the other crew, and trying to find out who's the one who's supposed to kill you if he dies."

"That's all you need, right? Once you find out, we can take that guy out and then Roman."

"It may be a little more complicated than that, but I have a plan. Until then, though, we cannot be seen together. It'll be like it was before."

"And after it's all said and done?" I ask, immediately wishing I hadn't.

"I don't know, Chevelley," he says sincerely. "I don't know."

And the truth is, I don't know either. It's been years. Years of me thinking so negatively of him, convincing myself that I hated him, and I don't know if it's possible to go back to that night on the Ferris wheel—before things went bad.

# CHAPTER 17

"OH MY GOD, CHEVELLEY!" GAGE exclaims as I walk into the house. He rushes towards me and pulls me into a tight embrace. "We've been so worried. How did you get away from him?"

"Don't worry, Chelle. We'll get that motherfucker!" Deacon hollers from the other side of the room.

I take a deep breath. "We have a lot to talk about."

"Did that asshole hit you?" Silas asks, coming around to inspect my face. "I'll fucking kill him!"

"How's Trax and Rem?" I ask, noticing their absence.

"Oh, they're fine. They're all bandaged up and resting."

"Good."

I drop to the couch, my entire mind and body feeling extremely exhausted. I just want to sleep, but I know I have to tell the guys everything I've found out.

"You need anything?" Gage asks.

"Some sort of pain reliever, please."

A minute later, I'm brought a glass of water and a bottle of pills. After I shake out three and swallow them down, I muster up the strength to talk to the guys.

"You've been gone for several hours. What happened?" Deacon asks.

"You guys aren't going to believe this story, but

please don't chime in with any of your smartass comments or whatever. For one, I'm not in the mood, and two, it won't help anything."

They nod with curious looks on their faces.

I don't know where to start, and I really don't want to tell the long version, so I go straight to the point.

"Xavier is playing Roman and has been all these years. He was basically coerced into joining up with him and playing along, because if he didn't, Roman would have killed me and my father."

I pause there, letting them take it all in.

"Uhh, okay," Gage says slowly.

"The day Roman killed his dad, Roman also told him that if he wanted to protect me, he'd have to protect him. If Roman was killed by us, or by Xavier—because he knew Xavier wanted him dead—then he had someone waiting to follow his order in killing me and Dad.

"He also knew that Xavier had nothing to fall back on job wise or money wise, so he said he'd teach him his business and make sure he had a job and money if Xavier worked for him. Xavier didn't really have a choice, but it took Roman years to trust X. They left town after it happened, that's why we didn't see them for a while. That's when Roman was training X."

Silas and Gage exchange looks. "I don't know if we should believe this. I mean, what if he's fucking with us?" Silas muses.

"I don't think he is."

"Yeah, but . . ." Deacon begins.

"But what, Deac?" I demand.

He pauses. "Are you being blinded?"

I'm up off the couch in a second. "No, I'm not being blinded. He explained everything to me, and I choose to believe him. If you don't want to, then fine! But, he's got a plan to finish this, and I want this to be over. We have to put our trust in him now. He's working that side of the team, and as soon as he can, he's going to bring it down. I don't have to explain myself to you, Deacon, so I suggest you don't ask me any other stupid questions."

The room goes quiet. I sit back down, waiting for my racing heart to calm down, and my anger to recede.

"By the way, he suspects Roman killed Dad, and he's looking into it to get proof." Everybody gives me the sympathy eyes, but I'm not in the mood to be emotional. "Roman's in the hospital, but he's going to live. While he's there, Xavier is going to try to get information from some of his guys. He wants to find out who has the order to kill me if Roman gets killed. If Roman dies before we find out who's in on his threat, then I'm as good as dead, too.

"And just so you all know, Xavier didn't kill Jasper or Jai. He shot Trax and Rem, but he knew his shots wouldn't be fatal. He just needed to slow them down, so he could get away without getting killed. If he dies, Roman doesn't have a reason to keep me alive. I'm alive, because my life means Xavier will continue to work for him. So, kill him if you want, but know that bullet takes two lives."

With that, I push past them and go to my room. I'm in dire need of rest, and I don't have the patience to deal with anybody right now. I have too much swimming around in my mind, and I can't seem to grasp any of it.

I run a hot bubble bath, not having the energy to even stand in the shower. Once my body is submerged in the water, I close my eyes and try not to think about anything.

Unfortunately, that doesn't last too long as thoughts begin shooting through my brain like bullets from a gun.

Xavier worked with Roman in order to protect me and my father.

Xavier's trying to find out who killed my dad.

Xavier threw away his relationships with everyone he knew, and has held back his rage against Roman all these years for me.

Xavier.

Xavier.

Xavier.

And, I've put so much energy into loathing him. Hating him for throwing what we had away. Being frustrated with him for working with the man who not only caused trouble for so many people, but who took his father away.

He's still a different man, though. Working with Roman and doing all the things he requires people do for him will make anybody a different person. He has to be a detached person now, especially since he's had to cut off his feelings just to be able to be near Roman for so long.

Now, I just have to wait for his guy Jimmy to find me when Xavier has any information. Since Roman doesn't know about Jimmy, it won't raise any red flags. Hopefully he's able to get information from Roman's guys regarding my father, and of course the man who's ready to take me down the moment Roman takes his last breath.

After cleaning myself up, I get out of the bath and throw on oversized T-shirt and a pair of boy shorts underwear. I comb through my dark, tangled hair before wrapping it up in a bun on the top of my head.

When I'm finally comfortable under my covers, I think back to that brief moment when I first saw Xavier after his father's death. It had been a couple years, and I had already come to the conclusion that I'd never see him again. I assumed he moved to get a fresh start somewhere else.

## *Past*

*"Do you want to grab something to eat?" Gage asks me while we're driving away from the hardware store.*

*"Yeah, sure. Dad's not gonna be home for dinner tonight, anyway. Where do you want to go?"*

*"Shake Shack?"*

*"Sounds good to me."*

*Gage and I enjoy our food while talking about football, going to the shooting range, and other random things. He makes me laugh while I'm drinking my shake, and I end up spitting some of it out on the table. I've always loved the closeness of our relationship. Gage isn't even one of my best friends, he's my brother. Nothing will ever come between us, and I love knowing I always have him to talk to.*

*"I'm gonna go to the bathroom before we leave," he says, getting up from the table.*

*"Okay. I'll meet you outside. I'm gonna have a smoke."*

*Once outside, I walk around to the side of the building and light up a cigarette. The street is busy, so I lean against the wall and people watch. A young couple dance on the corner while the man sings off key to his girl. She doesn't seem to mind that he can't sing, she's laughing and looking at him with such adoration. I can't help but smile while I watch them.*

*The light changes, and they're off crossing the road hand in hand. A man passes them, coming from the other side of the street. It takes me a second to focus in, but when I do, I can't help but say something.*

*"Xavier," I call out on instinct.*

*I can't believe he's here. My heart flutters with excitement.*

*He looks in my direction, but his look is anything but receptive. If I thought he'd be happy to see me after these past couple years, I was wrong.*

*Xavier looks around before swiftly walking over to me.*

*"Where have you been?" I ask right away. "Gage will be happy to see you're okay."*

*"It doesn't matter where I've been, and I couldn't care less who wants to see me. You will not be seeing me again. Do you understand?"*

*His eyes dance around like he's looking for someone. When they land back on me, he narrows them to slits.*

*"What's wrong with you?" I ask, my voice a small quiver.*

*"You don't need to worry about me. Worry about yourself, Chevelley. Being near me isn't going to do either of us any favors, so don't expect me to want to be around you like before. Things are different now." His voice is firm and icy.*

*My face contorts into a look of confusion. I study the man before me, and though he looks the same, he's anything but. He's hateful and rude. That's not the Xavier I knew.*

*"I see that." His eyes go over my shoulder, so I follow his gaze and find a man standing several feet away, watching us.*

*"Just watch your back, Chevelley. Okay? Watch your back."*

*Then he's gone. He walks past me, towards the man who was watching us. He stops to say something to him, but the man continues to stare at me. After a few seconds, Xavier turns around and looks at me one last time before they both walk away.*

***Present***

Looking back and examining our last encounter, I question every move and look of Xavier's. When he was looking around, did he know someone was watching him? That man that he walked to, was that one of Roman's guys? Did he have to be so rude because they were listening?

He told me that he and I being around each other wouldn't do us any favors. I understand that now, but then, I just thought he was being an asshole. *Watch your back.* Was he actually giving me a friendly warning rather than a threat like I assumed? Was it literal, because of the man who was actually behind me? Everything seems so different now.

After looking at the clock to see that it's two forty-five in the morning, I throw my arm over my eyes as I lie back on the bed. We only have until Roman recovers enough to be out of the hospital to not have to worry about too much. I imagine we've thoroughly pissed Roman off, so much so that he's going to want to be deeply involved in getting back at us. I don't think he'd send anybody to do a job he personally wants to do. So, I really need Xavier to find out as much as he can before then.

My phone chimes, and I jump from the bed to grab it off my nightstand. It's from a number I don't recognize which I've come to learn is always Xavier. He gets disposable phones pretty frequently.

> *I have news. Some good. Some bad. There's a guy who's worked for Roman for many years, and he's ready to retire. He has a hell of a lot of intel and doesn't mind talking now. I'm meeting with him tomorrow away from Roman's place.*

I respond as soon as I finish reading.

> *Great. So, what's the bad news?*

I get the dreaded pause between texts. He takes a few minutes before responding, and I stay staring at the screen for his next words to appear.

> *I'm coming over.*

My jaw drops and the air rushes out of my lungs.

> *Why? The guys aren't too accepting of your story. I'm*

*not sure it's the right time.*

*I'm coming over, Chevelley. I don't have a tail right now, so it needs to happen tonight. The news I have to tell you shouldn't be done through a text. Be ready for me.*

"Shit!"

I dash around my room trying to find clothes to throw on. It doesn't help that I haven't done laundry in a while. I end up finding a pair of high-waist black jeans and a black and white, loose crop top.

I leave my hair in a bun, and apply some ChapStick to my full lips before jogging down the stairs.

"Whoa, what are you doing?" Silas questions from the couch, giving me a once over.

"Where's Gage?" I ask, ignoring his question.

"In the kitchen," Gage yells out.

"Anybody else here?"

Silas narrows his eyes at me, probably noticing my panic. "No, Deacon left to check on Rem and Trax. Why? What the hell is going on? Why are you dressed? I thought you were asleep. It's like three in the morning."

I breathe a small sigh of relief at not having a house full of angry Xavier haters here, but Gage and Silas are probably the ones I need to worry about the most.

I wait until Gage walks into the living room. He's holding a toasted sandwich in one hand and a soda in the other.

"What's up, C?"

"Well, remember that stuff I told you earlier? About X?"

Silas rolls his eyes and Gage grunts. "Mmhhmm."

"Remember when I said that if you wanted to talk to him about his side of the story, he'd be willing to talk?"

"Get to it, Chevelley," Gage growls.

"Xavier is coming over."

"What!" Gage and Silas roar simultaneously.

"Look, he has news. He doesn't have anyone following him right now, so it's the only time he can come. He said he has to tell me something in person."

"You talk to him on the phone?" Gage questions, his jaw tense.

"He texted me. I don't have his number, but he knows mine since it's the same number I had several years ago."

"Why the fuck didn't he just tell you whatever he needs to tell you on the phone? We've been out all fucking night, and you just got away from him." Silas seethes.

"I told you! He said he needed it to be in person! And it's not like we're asleep. Stop worrying about the time."

Gage puts his stuff on the coffee table while making a chuffing sound. "You know what else needs to be done in person? Killing someone."

"Oh, Gage," I mutter in exasperation.

"I'm serious, C. I don't trust him anymore. I'm sorry."

"He's not coming to kill me."

"How do you know? This whole story of his could be a lie just to worm his way back in here and destroy us all."

"I just know, okay?"

"What kind of *news* does he have?" Silas asks skeptically.

"He already found a guy who's worked for Roman for a long time who's willing to talk. He said this guy has a lot of information."

"And this other news—this news that needs to be said in person, is something different?"

"Obviously."

"So, in the few hours that you've been away from him, he found new information?" Silas says, unconvinced.

The guys exchange a look that—to me—says this girl is making a stupid decision, and it sends me over the edge.

"You know what? It doesn't matter what you guys think. I'm giving you the courtesy of knowing that Xavier is coming to *my* house. I didn't have to tell you, but I didn't want to surprise you. I was being considerate. I don't need permission to do anything, okay?" I take a breath. "So, Xavier is on his way. He's going to come inside and he's going to tell me whatever he needs to tell me, and then he's going to leave. You can be here, or you can make yourself scarce."

I turn on my heel and walk out the front door. The cool, night air envelopes me, and I suck in a deep breath while lifting my face to the sky. The few stars that are visible sparkle in the soot colored sky like diamonds.

My phone chimes again, and the message tells me that Xavier is walking here from a block down and to make sure the gate is open.

I pull it open and a minute later, Xavier struts towards me. As much as I don't want to focus on his looks, it's kind of hard not to. He's the most attractive man I've ever seen.

He wears a dark gray button up under a black, leather jacket. His hands are in the pockets of his ebony colored jeans, and he walks like a man who doesn't have a care in the world.

"Chevelley," he greets, his voice warming me from head to toe.

"Xavier," I respond, just as formal.

His mouth turns up at the corner. "You wear that just for me?" he asks, pulling his hand out to gesture at my top.

I look down and see that it says, *I hate you.* A laugh bubbles up and explodes from my mouth, filling the quiet night.

"Uh. No, actually."

"That's good to know."

When we're inside the gate, I make sure to engage the lock, and then lead him to the front door.

"I'm not sure if Gage and Silas are gonna be in there or not. I told them you were coming over, and they weren't too happy."

He shrugs, unfazed, but then stops walking and grabs my elbow. I stop and turn back to look at him.

"What's wrong?" I ask.

"I know how much those guys mean to you, and I don't want my presence to mess anything up, but," he pauses and studies my face, "I don't care what they think or believe. It only matters to me what you think. I need to know that you truly believe what I'm telling you, Chevelley. If you think they'll be able to persuade you into thinking I'm lying, then there's no point in me being here. So, do you really believe me?"

I notice his hand is now encircling my wrist as he stares deeply into my eyes. I take a few moments to take in the sincerity painted on his face before I answer.

"I believe you, Xavier," I state confidently.

He nods. "I know I was friends with those guys before, but if they never believe what I'm saying, it won't affect my life. You understand what I'm saying?"

I nod, because he's telling me that it'll only affect him if I don't believe in him. And that in itself speaks volumes to me.

"Yes, yes. I understand," I say, finally finding my words.

"After you," he says, gesturing towards the door.

I walk in and am somewhat surprised to see Gage and Silas still sitting in the living room. Their eyes lift and meet mine before landing on Xavier behind me.

The heat in the room seems to be replaced with air as cold as ice. The three men eye each other speculatively, their bodies tense and on edge. I know none of them will say anything first, so I take that upon myself.

"Guys," I say cautiously. "Xavier has news. If you want to hear it, feel free to stay. If not, well . . ." I trail off, because they know where they can go.

"I think they should hear it," Xavier says firmly.

Gage's eyes narrow, and I can tell he wants to leave just because Xavier wants them to stay.

I take a seat on the middle cushion of the couch, next to Silas. Gage sits on the single chair to the right of Si, and I motion for Xavier to sit on my left, at the end of the couch.

He sits slowly, never taking his eyes off of the guys, and they do the same. It's obvious there's no trust in this room, which is understandable, we were just in a gun fight. It seems like it's been a lot longer than it actually has been. We were out there only about six hours ago.

"So, what's going on?" I ask, turning to face him.

He looks at me, but isn't able to hold my gaze. His eyes shift to Gage momentarily before looking down. He strokes his scruffy beard like he's in deep thought.

"It's about Memphis."

The guys seem to lean in at the mention of my father.

"What?" I ask, my voice a broken whisper.

"When I had Jimmy drop you off earlier, I met up with a man named Marco. He does business with Roman, but he's not on Roman's payroll. Marco is who Roman calls for cleanup when his normal guy isn't available."

The look he gives me when he says *cleanup* tells me

that Marco gets rid of bodies.

"I couldn't go to Roman's normal guy, because he's very loyal, so I took a shot with Marco. I questioned him under the ruse of Roman wanting some clarification. I made up a story as to why Roman would need more information regarding some of the bodies he discarded for him."

I flinch at hearing my father be referred to as a discarded body. Xavier places his hand on my knee for a moment, acknowledging my reaction.

"Turns out, Marco has only worked for Roman a handful of times. I pulled information from him regarding the victims, and what happened to them, and where they were . . . re-located to." He seems to choose his words carefully now.

"And?" I ask nervously, both wanting and not wanting to know.

"Your father was one of them," he answers, his voice laced with sympathy.

I never thought there was a chance my father could be alive, but now I know for sure that Roman was the one who killed him or had him killed. My body shakes as my anger rises when I think about how his body was just discarded. We were unable to have a proper funeral for that reason alone. Gage and I set up a funeral for him, but really, it was just a memorial, and only close friends were invited.

We knew he was dead when he never came home after leaving town for business. He had no reason to run off or fake his death, and he isn't the kind of person who would do that, anyway.

The thing with this business is knowing something like this could happen to any one of us. I just never imagined it happening to my father. To me, he was invincible.

"Where?" I manage to get out.

"Up near Willingboro."

Where he had business.

"I don't want details, but you know for sure?" I ask, my eyes boring deep into Xavier's honey brown ones.

The look that crosses his face lets me know he knows how he died, and there's definitely no doubt about it. "I know for sure," he answers softly with a small frown.

"And there's no way . . . I mean, we can't get . . ." I'm unable to finish my question, because a lump so thick forms in my throat.

Xavier seems to know what I was going to ask. He shakes his head, giving me a sympathetic look.

We can't recover his body, and that kills me. He'll never get a proper funeral. We can't even have him legally declared dead until several more years go by. We can't tell the cops we know how he died. This life prevents that.

My father was smart enough to have everything he owned put in my name as well, so I don't have to worry about that, but I'd gladly have nothing in my name to have my father back in my life.

"I didn't want to tell you this over the phone, and I know the guys," he gestures with his head towards Silas and Gage, but never takes his eyes off of me, "would want to know as well. I know this doesn't help or make anything better, but perhaps it gives you some closure, and you now know who made this happen. I promise Roman's going to pay for this. He's going to pay for taking both of our fathers away."

He grabs my hand and squeezes it in his. My eyes rest on our connected hands until his other hand grabs my chin and brings my head up to look at him. If I doubted him before, I don't now. The look in his eyes tells me he means everything he's saying. Killing Roman is just as important to him as it is to me.

"Thanks for letting me know," I tell him, giving his hand a slight squeeze.

"Of course."

I glance back at Gage and Silas who seem to have softened their faces a bit, but neither move to say anything.

"You'll let me know what happens with the guy you're set to meet tomorrow?" I ask.

"Yes. I'm now looking for the man who has the order to kill you. Once I find that out, I know what needs to be done. I will let you know either through text or via Jimmy when I find him." He pauses. "Because, I will find him, Chevelley. Don't doubt that."

"I know."

"Okay, well, I'm gonna get out of here while it's still dark." He gets up from the couch. "Even though Roman is still in the hospital, I'd be cautious when you leave the house."

I nod in acknowledgment and walk him to the front door. Right before he steps over the threshold, Gage gets up and calls his name.

"Hey, X." Xavier looks over his shoulder at him. "Thanks for letting us know about Memphis."

Xavier looks at me briefly before connecting eyes with Gage once again. He gives a single nod and then walks outside. I follow him out so I can be sure to lock the gate once he leaves.

Neither of us speak until we reach the gate.

"I think they'll come around," I say in regard to Gage and Silas.

"I may have to prove myself, but I'm not worried about it," he states confidently.

"Thank you for finding out about my father. I really appreciate it. I know you didn't have to look into it, because it didn't affect you directly, so thank you. Truly."

"It did affect me." I cock my head in confusion. "Watching my father die was the worst thing to happen to me, but you were right when you said at least I knew. I couldn't imagine going through everyday not knowing what happened or where he might be. I didn't want you to live like that any longer than you already had. I needed to give you that closure, no matter how painful, because the not knowing would eat at you."

The emotions that surge through me are conflicting. I never would have thought Xavier would have been so thoughtful, and care enough about how I felt, that he would go through this for me. It's a phenomenal feeling knowing somebody thinks about your feelings and emotions when contemplating a decision, especially if that decision can cost them their life. However, since I didn't think of him being so considerate, my heart hurts, because I was so wrong. The Xavier who still had his father was kind and selfless, but I thought that Xavier was long gone. I'm now realizing he's been here all along, just hidden deep inside a darker version of himself. A version he needed to become. But, he's always been the Xavier I loved.

Tears burn my eyes, but I will them back. "Thank you," I say again with as much sincerity as possible.

"You don't need to thank me, Chevelley. I've told you once before what I'd do for you, and I don't go back on my word."

I think back and remember a time when he said he'd do anything for me. I guess he was really telling the truth. It's easy to dismiss something like that when so often people promise such a thing, but are nowhere in sight when you actually need them. Xavier wasn't in sight, but he was definitely there for me. Watching my six.

A smile appears on my face at the thought.

"What?" he questions.

"Nothing. Just remembering something."

"Hmm," he murmurs, looking at me curiously. "Well, I guess I should be leaving."

"Be careful. There's criminals out there," I say with a small smirk.

"Then I suppose they should watch out for me." He winks at me and then he's walking away, disappearing into the shadows.

# CHAPTER 18

WHEN I WALK BACK INTO the house, Silas and Gage are in the midst of a conversation. They stop talking when I come in and give me a look I don't quite understand. I can't tell if they're angry or not, and I don't want to try to figure it out either.

"I'm going to sleep," I say, already walking to the stairs.

"Wait up, C," Gage says. With one foot on the step and my hand on the railing, I look back at him and wait. "We're sorry for being assholes earlier, but you understand why. We've all hated Xavier for a long time, because we thought he turned his back on us and didn't have the balls to tell us why. If he's telling the truth, I get it, but you gotta understand it's hard to get over it so quickly."

"I get it. I do."

"I really do appreciate him wanting to let us know about Memphis. That was a good thing for him to do."

"It was," I agree. "I'm really exhausted, guys. We can talk later, okay?"

They both nod.

"Of course," Silas states.

I trudge up the stairs, feeling like a zombie. Sleeping for twenty-four hours feels like a good plan to me.

As soon as my head touches the pillow, I'm out like a light.

ALL OF A SUDDEN I'M being pulled from my bed. My head slams against the floor with a loud thud, and spots fill my vision. My room is dim, and I'm unable to focus on anything around me. My brain seems to be taking some time to wake up, which is causing my reactions to be slow.

The first thought I do have is that Roman got out of the hospital and didn't waste any time to get his revenge. I think of Gage and Silas who I left downstairs. Are they okay? Did Roman kill them as soon as he got in?

A hard kick to my stomach flips me over causing me to curl into a fetal position and gasp for air. I stretch my arm out in front of me, trying to grab for a gun I know I keep under my bed. As soon as my fingertips graze the weapon, I'm forced onto my back with a black boot on my shoulder.

I stare up at the large figure who's cloaked in shadows, standing over me. I try to make out his facial features, but it's like he doesn't have any.

The man raises a gun, the chrome seems to shine brightly in the darkness. I watch as it's pointed directly at my head. The intruder has moved his foot to the middle of my chest, leaving me with no way to escape.

Ever so slowly, he inches towards me, his face gradually becoming more visible. Soon, I'm able to see who it is that's about to take my life.

His honey brown eyes meet mine and he grins.

"You thought I'd let you get away with trying to kill me?" he says ominously. "You should learn to listen to your friends, Chevelley."

"Xavier," I whisper in surprise.

He stands back up, his face disappearing into the dark once again, and then BAM.

I SIT UP STRAIGHT IN bed, my heart thundering hard in my chest like it's about to break through my skin and fall in my lap. My eyes roam the room looking for an intruder who isn't here.

The nightmare felt so real, and my body is still living in dreamland, because the fear and heartbreak is still strong in my body. Clearly, my subconscious is siding with Gage and Silas about Xavier.

A glance at the clock tells me it's already thirty minutes after noon. I feel like I didn't switch positions at all as I slept. My entire body is stiff, so I stretch my arms and legs before climbing out from under the covers and making my way to the bathroom.

After freshening up, the kitchen calls to me and my growling stomach. Surprisingly, neither of the guys are downstairs, and I saw their bedroom doors were open, so I know they aren't in the house. Once I put on a pot of coffee and pull out a carton of eggs, I pull the phone from the back pocket of my shorts and send a text to Gage to make sure they're okay.

His response is immediate, letting me know everything is fine. I put the phone on the counter and continue making my breakfast—even though it's lunch—burrito.

An hour later, I'm done eating and gathering laundry from our rooms. I only pick up whatever they've left on the floor, and leave everything else where it is. Once the clothes are in the washing machine, I turn my attention to the bathrooms, and then vacuum every room in the house.

I'm tightening up my ponytail as I head into the kitchen for a bottle of water. I spot my phone on the counter where I left it earlier and decide to glance at it. I find Gage had tried to get in touch with me a few times as well as Rem.

I'm in the process of calling Gage back as I walk into the living room when the front door is pushed open, and Gage and Silas walk through.

"Hey, we tried calling you," Gage says.

"Yeah, I know. I just saw that. I've been cleaning. Everything okay?"

"Yeah. We were with Rem and Trax."

"How are they?" I ask, resting my butt on the back of the couch.

"They're fine. Both of them are at Rem's place. We went and took them some food."

"We also told them about Xavier," Silas adds.

"Oh? What did you have to say?"

"I figured you wouldn't want to have the whole conversation with them, so we told them what Xavier told us last night, and everything you said he told you."

"And what did they have to say about that?"

"Pretty much the same stuff we said," Gage answers.

I make a noise at the back of my throat and roll my eyes. "I'm sorry I missed that."

"Rem wanted to talk to you. That's why we were calling," Silas says.

"He and X didn't really know each other that well, so all he knows is the bad stuff we had to say about him."

"Well, it didn't take him too long to get over it, surprisingly," Gage says.

"What do you mean?"

"We explained to him what Xavier told you about why he did and is still doing what he's doing. Working with Roman and all. He was skeptical, but when we told him about Xavier coming over and telling us about Memphis, he seemed to not question him anymore."

"Interesting," I say right as my phone begins ringing. "Speak of the devil," I say when I see Rem's name on the screen. "Hello?"

"Hey, C."

"Hey, Rem. How you feeling?"

"You know me. It's gonna take a lot more than a single bullet to the shoulder to take me down."

I laugh. "I know it."

"So, I heard about Xavier."

"Yeah."

"That bastard shot me," he says, but with a tiny bit of humor in his voice.

"I know he did."

"He didn't kill me, though, and he very well could have. I was out in the open with no cover."

"I know that, too."

"You trust this guy, C?"

"I believe his story, yes."

"I can understand his reasoning, and he wasn't really left with much choice, but if he's doing what he can to make sure you stay alive, then I can get on board with that."

"Really?"

"Of course. I mean, he owes me dinner or something for shooting me, but I can be patient."

I laugh. Rem may have a temper, but he has the best personality. He's a jokester, and I love that he can always make me laugh.

"I'll let him know about dinner. You want him to take you to a fancy restaurant?" I joke.

Rem laughs. "Nah. I'm not that high maintenance. Some takeout will do."

"It means a lot that you have my back on this, Rem. Thank you."

"I trust you, C."

"That means more than you know."

"If he screws us over, or hurts you in any way, I can't promise you that I won't hurt him."

"If that happens, I might do it myself."

"We can team up," he says lightheartedly.

"Sounds good," I laugh. "How does Trax feel?"

"Physically? He's fine. About this Xavier thing? He hasn't said much since Gage and Silas left. It'll be alright, though, C. Don't worry about it. Everybody will get on board."

"I wish I had your confidence."

"Well, we all know I'm the most confident person there is."

"Cocky," I murmur with an eye roll.

"Confident, C. Confident. There's a difference."

"Sure thing. Well, I'll let you get some rest. I'll talk to you soon."

"Alright."

"Take care."

"You know it."

After we disconnect, I move around to the front of the couch and fall into the cushion. A good chunk of relief comes over me now that I know Rem is on my side.

"So, are you guys still on the fence about Xavier and his side of the story?" I ask.

Gage sits on the other end of the couch, doing something on his phone, but he stops to look at me.

"We'll see what happens, C. I'll still be extremely cautious around him, but he did say a lot that made sense, and I don't think he'd come over and give us information about Memphis if he was trying to fuck us over. I remember the Xavier we were friends with. But, I also remember how quickly he became the Xavier we didn't understand and then the Xavier we hated. He might just be very good at flipping a switch and being whatever's necessary for the moment."

Silas is at the dining room table on the computer, but he closes the laptop and walks into the living room.

"You know I support you, Chevelley, in whatever decisions you make. You know Xavier in a way we don't. I'd say you know a lot more about him than anybody, at least on a personal level. If you truly believe that he's telling the truth and is willing to help us take down Roman, then I have no reason to doubt you. I don't see why he wouldn't want to see him dead. I never understood his working with him, but it makes sense now."

I give Silas a small smile. "Thank you." My eyes shift to Gage. "He's going to help us. All of us together are going to make sure Roman pays for what he did. We need to work together on this. You don't have to become his best friend, you don't even have to talk to him, you just can't kill him."

Gage gives a half snort half laugh. "I guess I can refrain from that."

I get closer to him and kiss his bearded cheek. "Thanks. I love you."

"I love you, too, C. That's why I worry."

"I know."

"I love you, too, Si," I say, standing up to give him a hug.

He squeezes me into a tight bear hug. "Love you, too."

The rest of the day goes by fast. I continue cleaning the house from top to bottom while the guys start getting dinner together. They said they're going to fire up the BBQ and I never say no to that.

I rush upstairs to shower when they start putting the

hamburgers on the grill. I feel like a giant dust ball covered in cleaning products, and I don't want to be smelling Lysol and bleach while I eat.

As soon as I get out of the shower and throw some comfortable clothes on, my phone rings.

"Hello?"

"Hey, Chevelley."

"Hey, Johnny. How's everything going?"

"Ah, you know."

I crack a smile, because Johnny always says that. *You know.* But, I don't. He doesn't talk about anything in his personal life, he doesn't complain, and he doesn't celebrate. Everything is always, *well, you know.*

"Yeah, sure. So, what's up?"

"I just got done talking to Mario and the Muccino brothers. Some crazy shit went down, huh?"

"Oh fuck. You didn't know? I thought Gage might have called you."

He sucks his teeth. "He did, he did, but he didn't give me all the details."

"Oh? Like what?"

"Like you being kidnapped."

I take a seat on my bed. "I wasn't kidnapped per se."

"Right. You aren't a kid. You were abducted."

I scoff, but let out a chuckle right after. "Johnny, I'm fine."

"See, this is why I need to be there for shit like this."

"No, you don't. You have a family, and Wanda would kill me if anything happened to you. Dad started recruiting younger, single men for a reason."

"Oh, you're saying I'm too old?" he asks without malice.

"Of course not. I know you still have it," I say with a laugh. "I'm just saying, you and Lou stay out of the really violent things now for a reason. Plus, I couldn't handle it if anything happened to you guys. With you still around, I feel like I still have a piece of my father."

He lets out a long sigh. "I know. I know. So, tell me what happened."

I recite everything that happened, starting from us arriving to the garage and ending when everything went black for me.

"I got Mario's version which started with them being inside and hearing a gunshot. Mario knew something must have went wrong, but he had no choice but to follow Roman and Xavier outside.

"He told me about how he saw Rem coming up with his gun aimed at Roman, but Xavier saw him before he could shoot. During the midst of the gunfire, Gage and Silas made sure to pull him and Micky—the guy he took with him—around to the other side, since they were the only ones with no weapons."

"Oh, I wondered what happened to them."

"They were in the garage trying to find loaded weapons. Everything Roman had was unloaded, which is smart, but left them with nothing to defend themselves with. Anyway, he said once he saw Roman drive off, they came around and saw Gage and Silas running into the building. Rem was struggling trying to get in touch with Deacon, and you disappeared around the other side of the building.

"When they yelled out that Trax was found inside, they all ran inside to see how he was doing. Rem sent a message to Deac, but apparently, by the time Deacon got the text, Roman had already passed him. He tried following him, but he ended up losing him due to traffic.

"So, Gage let you believe that I went inside to check on Trax with the rest of them?"

"Yep."

"Well, he probably didn't want you to worry."

"He knows better. He should have told me."

"How did you find out?"

"Isaac and Bobby told me."

"Oh. Xavier made them get out of the car."

"So I heard," he grunts.

"Johnny, I gotta tell you something. I'm not sure how you're gonna take it, but you need to know."

I hear him moving around and then he releases a loud sigh. "Alright. I'm sitting down. Give it to me."

Once again, I repeat the entire Xavier story. Johnny listens quietly, never interrupting me while I speak. Once I've said everything, I hear him clear his throat.

"I can't say I'm too surprised."

"Really?"

"Xavier was never a bad kid. I spoke to him several times back when he would be at your house pretty often. Nobody, including your father, thought badly of him. It's not really out of character for him to go to extremes for someone he cares about. Take his father for example."

"What do you mean?"

"He worked for his father because his father needed him. Xavier had plans to move away as soon as he was eighteen, but he didn't. He couldn't leave his father."

My bottom jaw drops a little. I had no idea that he didn't want this life. He's been sacrificing himself and his dreams for a long time now.

"I didn't know that."

"You wouldn't. He never spoke about it. One day, during a fight, he told his father that he resented him. Victor told me about it later. He felt guilty for holding his son back, and when he finally got to a point where he felt he didn't need him anymore, Xavier refused to leave."

"Why?"

"Don't know."

"So, you believe his story?"

"I do. Obviously, we were all confused about why he would want to work with Roman after Roman killed his dad, but that's not our business."

"I know that, but it seemed like he didn't want anything to do with us anymore, and every time I saw him, he went out of his way to be rude to me. He threatened me and my friends, and I couldn't understand how he could do that. I suppose I know now why he was doing it, but at the time, what was I supposed to think?"

"He never hurt you."

"He hurt my heart," I say softly.

Johnny stays quiet, possibly feeling uncomfortable about my admission.

"He had to do that to keep you safe. He's saving your life, Chevelley."

"I know."

"And he tried to save your father's as well. It's commendable."

At the mention of my father, I remember something.

"Hey, Johnny. Do you know if my father was doing business with Roman right before his death?"

"He had a lot of things going on at the time of his death, but doing business with Roman is something I don't think he'd do. He hated Rome for what he did to Victor. Roman had called him and demanded he supply the guns he wanted when Victor didn't have them in time, but you know your father didn't want to get mixed up with that stuff. After Roman killed Victor, he called your dad and told him that the blood was on his hands. Later that day, Memphis got a package with Victor's hand in it."

Chills run up my spine at the thought. I wonder if Xavier knows he did that.

"So, it's possible my dad was planning some sort of revenge?"

"He could have been, but I don't know for sure. If he was planning to do anything to him, I didn't know about it."

"Well, Xavier's meeting with someone who has a lot of information about Roman. Hopefully he finds out who Rome trusts the most, because it's likely that person will be the one who has the order to kill me."

"You let me know when you find anything out, and in the meantime, I'll dig around and try to figure some shit out. I know people who've worked with Rome in the past, but a lot of people aren't likely to give out information on him."

"Well, don't do anything that can get you on his radar."

"Of course."

"I'll talk to you soon, Johnny."

"Tell that boy me and him are gonna have some words," he says gruffly, talking about Gage.

"I will."

He grunts. "Alright, then."

We disconnect and I flop back on the bed with a loud sigh. The door to my room is pushed open.

"What the hell? The food's getting cold," Silas says when he sees me lying on the bed.

"I just got off the phone with Johnny."

Silas grimaces. "He found out about what happened to you?"

"Yep. The Muccino brothers told him."

"He pissed?"

"He said him and Gage are gonna have words."

"So, I take it you told him about X?"

"Yeah. Hey, did you know that my dad got a package with Victor's severed hand in it?"

"What?" Silas exclaims with wide eyes. "I never heard about that."

"Me either. Apparently my dad kept that between him and Johnny. Lou might know, too, but I had no idea."

"He probably kept a lot to himself." I nod. "Well, come downstairs and eat."

Silas pulls me up off the bed, and we saunter down the stairs towards the aroma of burgers and hotdogs.

I warn Gage about the call he's gonna get from Johnny.

"I just didn't want to tell him until I knew something for sure," he tries to defend.

"You ain't gotta tell me," I say, holding up my hands. "He just wants to be in the loop at all times."

All three of us enjoy our food and have a couple beers afterwards. When they start watching some old movie I'm not interested in, I wander into my dad's office. I feel the need to be around his things. He spent most of his time in the office, even falling asleep on the couch in here rather than going to his room.

I took his room when he died, not being able to imagine anybody else staying in there. Gage took mine, and Silas stayed where he was. Jasper didn't move in until after my father's death, and he got Gage's old room. Eventually, we'll have to clear it out, even if nobody uses it.

I sit in the old, leather chair that's had the seat squashed flat. It used to be full and comfortable, but my father sat in it so often, and he wasn't a slight man. The poor cushion is flat as a pancake now.

An autobiography of a hitman who worked for the mob sits on the edge of his desk. A picture of me at the age of about six rests in the upper corner, and in the opposite corner is a photo of both of us when I was about sixteen. I pick up the frame and study it. My father's sitting on the couch, and I'm leaning over his shoulder, my hands resting on his shoulders, and my cheek pressed against his.

A tear falls down my cheek as a small smile touches my lips.

"I love you, Daddy," I whisper before putting the frame back in its place.

I allow myself a few minutes to grieve. I grieve for my father. The man who lost his life trying to set things right. I mourn my two friends, Jai and Jasper. Men who had my back and were always there for me. And, I weep for Xavier. The man who's still alive, but living in a life he never wanted. A life that took away the two people he cared about the most.

I just cry.

# CHAPTER 19

XAVIER CALLS AS I'M CLIMBING into the bed.

"Hello?"

"Hey, it's Xavier."

"I know. You're the only who calls from unknown numbers."

"Are you okay?" he questions.

"Yeah." I clear my throat. "Why?"

"You just sound different."

I'm amazed he's even able to tell. I suppose I didn't hide the sorrow in my voice very well.

"I'll be okay. So, what's going on? Did you find the guy?"

"No, I didn't," he replies, his voice full of regret. "But, the guy I spoke to gave me a lot of information about Roman and his operation. Things I haven't been privy to. I have a plan."

"Are you going to tell me?"

"I'm not sure you're going to like it."

I scoff. "Xavier, will you please tell me? I don't like a lot of shit, but I can deal with it."

"Let me make sure it's doable first. If it is, then I'll fill you in."

"Fine." I huff and roll over onto my side with the phone still pressed to my ear.

"Are you sure you're okay?"

"I'm a big girl, Xavier. I don't need to be coddled."

"I know you are, but you don't have to pretend like you don't have emotions. Being void of them isn't a good thing, Chevelley. I know a lot of time has passed, but I still remember you. I know everything you feel, you feel deeply and passionately. And you should know I'm not the coddling type."

"What type are you?"

"I don't know. You'd have to find that out for yourself."

Maybe it's the comfort of being alone in my room. Perhaps being under the covers in the dark sparks some bravery in me, but I ask the question that's been on my mind recently.

"Will I have the chance to figure out who you are now?"

Silence.

My confidence goes out the window. It feels like time stands still and I almost want to hang up and forget this conversation ever happened.

"I'm not sure you'll like what you find out."

"Maybe I will."

He sighs. "I'm not a good person, Chevelley."

"I'm not the greatest person either. Perhaps it's you who won't like what you see in me."

"We're both different now."

"I know," I agree.

"You tried to kill me."

I grimace at his words. "I thought you were trying to kill me and I thought you killed my friends."

"You broke into my house."

"You lied to me."

"You were going to kill me while I slept."

"You shot Rem and Trax."

"None of that beats the fact that you wanted me dead and were going to do it yourself."

"I never *wanted* you dead!"

"Oh? I find that hard to believe."

"In my moment of grief and anger, yes, I wanted you dead. Only because I thought you were responsible for what happened. Before then, I just wanted the Xavier I lo . . ." I pause and re-think my words, "I actually liked to come back. I wanted to understand you and the things you were doing. I wanted you to want to be around us . . . me again."

"I can't become the old me again. It's not possible. I am who I am now. You and everybody else are going to have to accept that."

I let out a long sigh. "Maybe we are too different now. Too much time has gone by, and too many things have happened. I'm gonna go, Xavier."

He lets out a low growl before hanging up.

God, why did I even open my big mouth?

Oh, I know. Because, I'm a fucking dumbass. I let my emotions get the better of me. He says being void of them isn't a good thing, well, when you let them make decisions for you, it's a terrible thing.

I still have feelings for Xavier. That may be fucked up, but it is what it is. He's the only guy I've been romantically involved with that I cared about. The only one who won't run scared when they find out what I do and who I live with. He's not threatened by the guys in my crew. He's the only one who makes me feel like a woman.

"Fuck," I growl, flipping to my stomach and burying my face in the pillow.

I end up tossing and turning before getting comfortable enough to fall into a deep sleep. It feels like I only get a few minutes of that good, uninterrupted, deep sleep when my phone starts dinging. My eyelids feel heavy as I try opening them. It takes several tries to get them open enough to focus on my phone's screen. The first thing I look at is the time. It's ten minutes after two in the morning. I probably fell asleep around twelve forty-five.

The phone dings again.

*Get Gage and Silas and meet me at 8584 Marshall Rd. Lansdowne.*

*Right now.*

What the fuck? It's two in the morning and I'm exhausted. I want to pull the covers over my head and go back to sleep, but I know I can't. I just wish Xavier would give me more information.

*Why? What's going on?*

It takes him a couple minutes to respond. While I wait, I pull on some black jeans, and a black Rolling Stones shirt. I walk across the hall to Gage's room and knock lightly before opening the door.

"Gage. Get up," I say, walking towards his bed. He doesn't budge. "Gage!" I yell while giving him a good shake. "Come on. You gotta wake up."

"Huh?" he murmurs, looking around the room with glazed over eyes.

"Xavier needs us to meet him in Lansdowne."

"That's like half an hour away. What time is it?"

"A little after two. Get up."

"Fuck!" he snarls, pushing the blankets off of him.

I walk out of his room and into Silas.'

"Oh yeah, yeah. Fuck me. Oh, God," a girl moans

from Si's bed.

"Uhh. Silas, we gotta go," I say, turning my head to the side, so I don't have to see his bare ass while he thrusts inside this woman.

"C, what the fuck?"

"It's important. We're meeting X in Lansdowne. Now."

I close the door and go back to my room to put on my shoes. My phone is lit up, so I glance at the screen.

*Can't text. Driving. You better be on your way.*

"Texted long enough to say that," I mumble to myself.

A few minutes later, Silas is putting some redhead into her car. Me and Gage climb into his truck and drive out the gate, waiting for Silas to lock it up. When he climbs in, we take off towards the small borough of Lansdowne.

"Now, can someone please tell me why the fuck we're headed thirty minutes away at two in the goddamn morning?" Gage snips.

"X texted me and told me to get you two and drive to some address there. He didn't give specifics."

"And we're just going in blind? Xavier says something and we do it without knowing what the fuck we're getting ourselves into? Sounds like a great plan," he says sarcastically.

"He was driving and couldn't divulge any more information. I imagine it has to do with Roman or the guy he's been trying to find. Maybe he found out where he was."

"And, maybe not," Gage responds coolly.

I ignore his attitude and stare out the front window. We're fifteen minutes onto Route 13 when a car from the other side of the road veers into our lane. Luckily for us, the car is about a half a mile away, but unfortunately, it slams into a jeep, creating what looks like a three or four car collision.

The traffic slows, and we end up only yards away from the debris. A tire rolls down the street, broken glass covers the road, and shards of metal liter the area.

There's no way we're going to get past this anytime soon.

Gage and Silas get out to go check on the people involved in the crash. I call the cops to inform them of the accident and am told they already have people on the way. Knowing Xavier is gonna be waiting on us, I shoot him a text.

> *Bad accident. We're stopped on Route 13 with no way to get around.*

Forty minutes go by before the cops are able to open up a lane for us to get by on. Xavier never wrote back, but we still make our way to the address he gave us.

We pull up in front of a small, red brick building with black trim.

"Is this a bar?" Gage questions.

"Looks like it."

"Is he still here?" Silas asks.

I go to my phone and ask him the same question. I get my answer when he steps outside. Xavier looks around until Gage flashes his lights from across the street, grabbing his attention. He walks over, looking like every woman's wet dream. His hair is unruly, yet perfect. All he has to do is run his hand through it to keep it in place. The hair over his lip and across his jaw line is the perfect length. My stupid, girly heart does flips at the sight of him. I remember our conversation just hours ago and do my best to ignore him when he comes to Gage's window.

"The guy Roman has ordered to kill Chevelley was here. His name is Junior. He left already, though," he says as soon as the window is down.

"Why didn't you kill him?" Gage asks bluntly.

"Couldn't. He was with a group of people. It wasn't the right time, especially since I was by myself. I wanted you all to see him, so you knew who to watch for. I know who he is now, though, and that's good. Plus, I have my guy Jimmy following him now. Hopefully he leads him to his house."

"Well, fuck. If that accident hadn't slowed us down, we might have been able to take care of him tonight," Silas says.

"We're getting closer," Xavier offers.

"Well, might as well not waste the trip out here," Gage says, pulling the keys out of the ignition.

I finally look in his direction, catching sight of Xavier behind him. "We're staying?"

"Might as well get a drink and some food before driving back."

"Well, I'm staying in here. I'm tired."

"That's not a good idea," Xavier says.

"Yeah, you're not staying out here by yourself," Gage agrees.

"You know what, guys? I'm a . . ."

"Big girl," they all say simultaneously.

"Yeah, we know," Gage deadpans. "But, you're coming inside. We won't stay for long, but I'm fucking hungry now."

I let out a frustrated growl and start sliding towards Silas. "Well, come on." We're almost to the door when I say, "I'm surprised you even want to be around this guy," I say, jerking my thumb towards Xavier.

Nobody says anything, but I swear I hear Xavier let out a low laugh. I walk ahead of them, and find a place at the bar. The bartender—an older man with greasy hair and a paunch stomach—gives me a once over and a creepy grin.

"Hey, little girl. You lookin' for a daddy?"

I narrow my eyes at him and am about to go off when Xavier, Silas, and Gage find their places around me.

"You lookin' for a bullet in your head?" Xavier snarls.

The bartender looks at the large, intimidating men and wisely backs off. He walks to the other side and tells the second bartender to tend to us.

"No bar that's open past 3am is a good place to be," I murmur.

Xavier and Silas both get Jack and Coke, I get Captain Morgan and Coke, and Gage settles for a beer since he has to drive us back soon. The bar has a small menu, so we each order some variation of a burger and fries.

Silas sits on my right at the curved end of the bar, both of us taking up the only two seats on this side, and Gage and Xavier sit to my left, allowing us all to see each other.

"So, do you think this Junior guy is the only one who Roman told about Chevelley?" Silas asks, breaking the silence.

"I'm pretty sure he is," Xavier answers.

"*Pretty* sure?" Gage repeats.

"Do you have any helpful information?" Xavier retorts.

Gage doesn't respond, but his jaw clenches in annoyance. Xavier has a point.

"Is Roman still in the hospital?"

"Yeah, I saw him earlier. He'll be getting out soon, so the sooner we can get rid of Junior, the better."

"You went and saw him in the hospital?" Gage asks between clenched teeth.

"Yes, I did, Gage. I'm doing my part in this whole

fucked up situation. What're you doing?"

"Making sure you aren't here to screw us over."

I roll my eyes.

Xavier looks at Silas. "Jimmy should be getting in touch with me soon to let me know what he finds out. As soon as I know, I'll let you know what the plan is. However, if the opportunity comes up for me to take him out, I will, and then let you know afterwards."

Silas nods. I let my eyes move to the left and catch a quick glimpse of Xavier. He's looking right at me. I immediately focus on my food.

"You're awfully quiet, Chevelley," Xavier taunts.

"Yeah, it's weird," Silas says.

"I don't have anything to say."

"Really? Even though we're talking about the guy who has orders to kill you?" X questions.

"I'm not in a good mood," I exclaim. "Some fucking asshole pissed me off earlier and I didn't get much sleep. Leave me the fuck alone."

Xavier's lips curl up slightly, giving me an amused smile. "Who's the asshole? What'd he do?"

I narrow my eyes at him. I'm not having this conversation in front of Gage and Silas, so I keep quiet.

"Are you seeing someone, C?" Silas asks, oblivious to what's really going on.

"No, Si. I don't think anybody can handle me."

"You scaring them off like you scared off the girl I brought home?" Silas asks with a grin.

I laugh. "No. I guess they don't know how to deal with me and everything that comes with me."

"Like us?" Silas questions.

"Something like that. One day a real man will come along and won't be afraid to take what he wants."

I lift my drink to my mouth and let my eyes find Xavier. He looks pissed.

"Relationships are overrated, anyway," Silas says. "Just find someone to get some ass from. It's less complicated."

"What makes you think I haven't found one of those already?" I say with a smirk.

"Oh really?" Silas asks, lifting both his brows.

I shrug. I'd never tell them about Rem, but I just want to get under Xavier's skin.

"Chevelley, please. I don't want to hear about your sexual escapades," Gage mumbles.

"Sorry," I say with a laugh.

Gage likes to live in a fantasyland where I don't know anything about sex. It's the big brother in him.

I finish my drink and then hop off the stool. "I gotta go to the bathroom. Make sure that creeptastic bartender doesn't follow me."

The bathroom is surprisingly clean and doesn't smell like shit. However, I think I'm the only female in the bar, so I guess it doesn't get used too often.

When I exit the stall, I wash my hands, and pull my hair from the ponytail holder. I comb through the thick locks with my fingers and leave it loose.

The door to the bathroom swings open just as my hand touches the knob.

"Jesus Christ!" I exclaim as I barely dodge getting hit in the face. I lay eyes on Xavier, because who else would it be? "What're you doing in here?"

"Taking what I want," he growls before pushing me further into the bathroom and up against the wall.

His mouth clashes with mine and I open it up to him immediately. I feel his whiskey flavored tongue caress mine. His kiss intoxicates me, making me feel dizzy and sending warmth through my body.

"Stop," I moan into his mouth. I push at his chest until he steps back. "We already said we can't do this.

We're too different."

"You said nobody can handle you, but that's bullshit. I'm the *only* one who can handle you. I think you know that, and I think you hate it."

"You can't handle me, Xavier!" I argue.

"Stop lying to yourself. I know how to deal with you and everything that comes along with you. I've done it before. Those fucking guys out there don't scare me. I'm not a little boy, Chevelley. I'm a fucking man, and I'm the only man you want. Just admit it. You want me as much as I want you. The only reason you haven't found someone is because you're looking for me in every single one of them. Well, there's only one of me, and I'm standing right here."

He doesn't give me time to respond, because his mouth is on mine again. He kisses me with force and with passion. He wraps my hair in his hand and tugs on it, exposing my neck to him. He kisses the flesh below my ear before catching it between his teeth. I moan out loud and run my fingers through his hair.

His large hands grip my waist and he pulls me into him, allowing me to feel his growing erection. I try my hardest not to rub myself on him, but I'm not sure I succeed. Once again our mouths connect, both of our tongues twirl around each other's in perfect harmony. I tug on his hair while his hands roam my body.

He lifts me up by my ass and I wrap my legs around his waist. I feel his cock pushed right up against my pussy, and this time I don't care that I grind myself on him. He grunts and I moan. I suck on his tongue and he bites down on my bottom lip. We're completely lost in the moment; completely lost in each other.

"Xavier," I pant.

"You want me, Chevelley?" he asks.

"Yes," I breathe huskily.

"C! Are you okay?" I hear Gage yell through the door.

"Goddammit," I hiss, sliding down from Xavier's body. "Uh, yeah. I'm fine. I'll be out in a minute."

He doesn't respond, so I assume he just walked away. Xavier runs his hand through his hair, putting it back in place. I go to the mirror and end up putting my hair back in a ponytail. My lips look a little more red and swollen, but there's nothing I can do about that.

"Umm. I'm not sure if we should let them know what went on here," I say a bit awkwardly. "I don't even know what went on."

He smirks at me. "That's fine. I'll go outside through the back exit and say I had to take a phone call. You guys meet me out front."

"Okay."

He gives me a cocky grin, looking me up and down one last time before walking out of the bathroom.

I let out a long breath and count to ten before I leave and meet up with Gage and Silas at the bar. They both give me a funny look when I approach.

"What?"

"What took you so long?" Gage asks.

"I didn't know I had to discuss my bathroom activities with you. Maybe I started my period. You wanna talk about it?"

Gage makes a face. "Uh no."

"Come on, let's go. Did you pay yet?"

"Yeah, I just paid," Silas answers.

"Where's Xavier?" I ask, trying to sound genuinely curious.

"He said he was gonna make sure nobody followed you into the bathroom, and then use it himself."

I almost laugh out loud. He made sure nobody except him followed me inside. "Well, I'm going to the car. I can text him."

When we step outside, Xavier's coming around the corner with the phone pressed to his ear.

"Yeah, okay. See you soon." He puts the phone in his pocket and approaches us. "Sorry about that. I got a phone call. You guys heading out?"

"Yeah, it's late and we need to get back home," Silas replies.

"I'm leaving, too. I'll be in touch later with whatever information Jimmy got about Junior."

I nod my head. "Okay."

"Alright, man," Silas says. He seems to be becoming comfortable with X again. He's not the only one.

He gives me a slight smirk before walking towards the small lot across the street and getting into his car. The three of us pile in the truck, and I immediately close my eyes, hoping the guys don't talk to me. I want to be lost in my own thoughts about Xavier and try to work them out.

The thing that keeps nagging me the most is what he said about looking for him in everybody I dated. Now, I didn't date a whole lot of people, but he's right. I compared every single one of them to Xavier, and none of them even came close. Rem is the only guy I've been with who isn't frightened by my lifestyle, because it's his, too. But, as much as I like Rem, I know we'd never last. We're great friends, and we'd do anything for each other, and I'd be a liar if I said he wasn't attractive, but he doesn't ignite in me the things Xavier does.

In our conversation before, Xavier seemed to make it clear nothing could work between us, or was that me? I don't even know anymore.

The next time I open my eyes, we're at home and Silas is shaking me by the shoulder.

"Mm. What time is it?" I ask groggily.

"After five," Silas answers.

I groan and force myself out of the truck. All of us drag ourselves upstairs and fall into our beds.

At eleven o'clock my phone wakes me up once again. I blindly reach for it and answer without even opening my eyes.

"Hello?" There's no hiding my gravelly, sleep-filled voice.

"Good morning, sleeping beauty," Xavier's suave voice replies.

"Ugh. Do you ever sleep?"

"Not really, no. It's especially hard now since when I sleep people like to break into my house."

"Not again," I groan.

I hear him chuckle. "I have news."

"What is it?"

"Roman's getting out of the hospital tomorrow."

My body wakes up a little more at the news. "What time?"

"Not sure yet."

"Did you find out where Junior lives?"

"He didn't go home. He went to Roman's house."

"Of course he did. Why don't all of his people just move in with him?" I ask, annoyed that we don't have an angle on him yet.

"Well, that's sort of my plan. Not to have people move in with him, but to get everybody at his house."

"And then?"

"And then . . . boom. Everybody's gone."

"How so?"

"Don't worry about it. I have it figured out."

"Xavier, I want to be involved. He killed my father. I want to watch him take his last breath."

I hear him let out an exasperated sigh. "I don't know how to get you there without everybody seeing you. If they see you, the plan goes out the window."

"Well, you're smart. Figure something out."

"You're frustrating, you know that?"

"I've been called worse."

"I don't doubt it."

"Asshole," I murmur.

"Yeah, I know. So, Roman mentioned wanting a meeting with all his closest confidants at his house as soon as he gets out. He wants to discuss how to go about killing all your friends. He never mentioned killing you to me, because even though he believes I've come to enjoy working with him, he knows he has me in his pocket because you're alive. He won't tell me his plan to kill you, but don't doubt that that's his plan. He won't let you live after what happened at his garage. I'm going to invite everybody to his house, not just the top ones. He'll be confused as to why everyone is there, but by then it will be too late."

"If he knows that by killing me, you won't work for him anymore, why would he do it?"

"At this point, he doesn't care. You can't try to kill him and think he'll let it pass. And, I'm sure he thinks I'll stick around anyway, because who and what else will I have? He doesn't know that I have money. I've been saving, and I don't live lavishly. The only good thing that came from working with Roman was making connections. I have no doubt that there are multiple opportunities out there for me, plus I'll be able to do things the way I want to do them, because I'll be my own boss."

"Sounds like you have it all figured out."

"Not all of it, but most."

"Will you please try to find a way for me to be there?" I ask again.

After a few seconds and a small sigh, he says, "I'll try."

"Okay. I'm going back to sleep now."

"We'll talk soon."

We hang up and it doesn't take long for me to fall back asleep. Once again, I'm woken up by someone shaking me.

"C, wake up. Hey, C. Get up."

I moan and turn over, bringing the covers over my face. "Leave me alone," I mumble.

"Can't. You gotta get up."

"Gage. I love you, but I will fucking shoot you if you keep messing with me."

I hear laughter.

"Chevelley, it's fucking six o'clock. You've slept all day."

"Well, I keep getting woken up by phone calls and dragged into another town at stupid thirty in the morning. Can I sleep? Ever?"

"Fine. Should I tell your visitor to wait up here or downstairs?"

I pull the covers off my head, but I'm still facing the wall. "What visitor?"

"The asshole who keeps waking you up," Xavier's voice answers.

I flip around to see Gage and Xavier staring at me with amused faces. I quickly try to tame my wild bed-head.

"Oh. Um."

Gage stares at me for a moment and then looks at Xavier. "I'll be downstairs."

"Chevelley," Xavier greets with a crooked grin.

"Give me a second," I say, scrambling from the bed, pulling out some clean clothes from my dresser, and rushing into the bathroom.

I wash my face, brush my teeth, and comb out my terribly crazy hair. I put it in a loose side braid, and strip off the clothes I fell asleep in when I came home. The clothes I pulled out of the dresser end up being a pair of white-washed denim shorts, and a white tank-top.

Five minutes later, I emerge from the bathroom, feeling a little better about myself.

"Well, a warning would be nice," I say.

Xavier sits on the edge of bed, looking around the room. "Sorry. It wasn't really a planned visit."

I slowly walk to my bed and choose to sit as far away from him as possible. When he turns and looks at me, he takes in the obvious space between us and gives me a smirk.

"So, why did you come? And, I thought you always had someone watching you. What are they gonna tell Roman?"

"Well, first, I've been here for a little while. I was talking to the guys downstairs before coming up here."

My eyes widen in surprise. "Really? Talking to Gage and Silas?" He nods. "That's . . . surprising. How did that go?"

"We're all still alive," he says seriously as he shrugs one shoulder.

I laugh out loud. "Always a good thing. So, what about the tail?"

He regards me for a moment. "I took care of that." He continues to watch me, waiting for my reaction.

"You killed him." I say without question.

"I did," he nods. "He was making things difficult."

"What if Roman finds out?"

"If he finds out, it won't matter."

"I see. Well, why did you come over?"

He tilts his head at narrows his eyes slightly. "You don't care that I killed that man?"

"I've killed men before, too. Do you care about that? We do this. It's not morally right, but we don't live in a moral world. It's us or it's them. We kill or we're killed. Nobody would understand that unless they lived our lives. I believe you only killed him because you felt it necessary and not just for kicks."

"Well, alright then."

"Again. Why are you here?"

"We need to talk, Chevelley." His voice is serious.

"Talk about what?" I ask.

"If everything goes as planned tomorrow, we won't be under the thumb of Roman anymore. No need to put on these fronts, no hiding, no more lies. We'll be free to do whatever we want."

"Uh-huh," I murmur, anticipating where he's going with this.

"What is it you want to do?" he questions.

Ninety percent of me is sure he's talking about us, but I don't want to assume and embarrass myself. Last time I tried talking about us, he shut me down with talk of us being different people. "What . . . what do you mean?" I ask cautiously.

He gives me a knowing look. "I think you know."

"Xavier, last time I tried talking to you about us getting to know each other, you tried scaring me off by saying you're not a good person, and how we're different people now. What changed in such a short amount of time?"

He scoots closer to me. "I've come to realize that while we're both different than what we used to be so many years ago, we're still very much the same person. You understand?" I furrow my brows in confusion. "You and I are the same, Chevelley. We grew up, experienced more, lived through tragedies, caused tragedies, and a whole lot more, but are we not similar?"

"I think I know what you're saying," I say slowly.

"Our minds and our hearts are at war with each

other, because we're telling ourselves one thing while our hearts are feeling something else entirely. We may not be the best people in the world, but . . ."

"We're the best people for each other," I finish.

He gives me a small smile. "We understand each other on more than one level."

I nod. "I understand."

"Good."

"So . . ."

His phone rings, interrupting our conversation. When he looks at the phone, his brows furrow.

"Be quiet, okay?" he tells me.

I nod.

"Hello? Yeah. Right now? Okay. Yeah. I'll tell everybody. See you soon." He hangs up the phone. "Shit!"

"What?"

"Roman's getting out of the hospital right now. Not tomorrow. The meeting has been moved to an hour from now."

"What? Are you gonna be able to go through with your plan?"

"Everybody's still showing up for the meeting. I just have to get over there to get my shit in order."

"What about me? Do I get to come?"

He huffs. "I'm going to go first. You, Gage, and Silas can park two blocks away from his house. Stay hidden. I'll text you from inside the house."

"Okay," I nod.

"I gotta go," he says, walking to the door.

"Be careful," I call after him.

He pauses and looks at me over his shoulder. "You worried about me?"

I playfully roll my eyes. "Just be careful."

"You got it."

Xavier leaves the house in a hurry and I tell Gage and

Silas the plan. We leave the house ten minutes later. If everything goes smoothly, this war ends tonight.

# CHAPTER 20

WE'RE SITTING IN THE TRUCK a block and a half from Roman's house when I get a text from Xavier.

> *When it's time, I'm going to call you. Do not say anything. This is so you can hear what's happening. The phone will be in the breast pocket of my jacket, and that's the best I can do. I'll let you know how and when to make your way up here.*

I text back letting him know I understand, and continue to wait. It's about twenty minutes until everybody is supposed to be in place for the meeting. Nobody should be driving along the road we're on, so we won't know just how many people will be there.

My knees bounce up and down with nerves while I wait for the call.

"Do you know his plan?" Silas asks me.

"No." I wait a few minutes before I speak again. "What did you and Xavier have to talk about earlier? He said he was downstairs for a while."

"He retold the story he told to you. I guess he wanted to make sure we knew everything," Silas states.

"We talked about the day his father died and the subsequent days that followed. Roman was certain to make sure Xavier had no other options but to work under him," Gage joins in.

"So, you came around?" I ask Gage.

"When you hear the details from him, it's hard to not believe."

Silas nods solemnly. "You should know something, Chevelley," he starts.

Gage shoots him a stern look. "Is this really the best time to have this conversation?"

"What?" I ask, looking between the two.

Silas glares back at Gage before softening his gaze and looking at me. "Xavier did something, and it's something I think you should know about."

Gage huffs and looks out the driver's side window. "It could wait."

"Well, spit it out! You're freaking me out."

He takes a deep breath and releases it slowly. "He . . ."

My phone blares, startling me. "Shit. You guys have to be quiet."

I answer the phone and immediately have it on speaker. It takes a minute before I hear any voices.

"What's going on?" a muffled voice asks. It's not Xavier's. The voice continues to talk, but I can't quite make anything out. He's obviously not very close to Xavier.

"Don't worry, we'll be back upstairs in time for the meeting," Xavier answers calmly.

"We don't have that long, what do you need to tell me, Xavier?" The angry voice spits. It's Roman's voice.

"It has to do with the men who were shooting at you."

"Oh?" Roman says with interest.

"Yes. While you were in the hospital, I was able to work my way back in and lie to them about where my loyalties lie. They trust me now. Well, mostly. The bastards aren't trying to kill me, anyway," he laughs.

"You're talking to them?" Roman booms in bewilderment.

"Calm down, boss. Here, sit down and take it easy. You still aren't completely healed."

"Why didn't you tell me what you were doing?" he demands.

"I needed to make sure I could do it first. I didn't want to take something to you that wasn't a sure thing. Now, I can get these guys to a place of your choosing, and we can take them all out at the same time."

"Huh," Roman grunts. "What about the girl?"

"What about her?" Xavier asks, and I can tell his teeth are clenched.

"She was there that night, too."

"I know. I did my best to keep her from shooting you."

"Did you?" Roman questions.

"Yes, I did. Do you not believe me? I've threatened and warned her several times about what would happen if she messed with you. I told her I wouldn't allow it."

"If that's the truth, I'm impressed. I know she had you wrapped around her finger for a while."

"Yeah, well, I was young. I've since learned I don't need some bitch ruining my life."

Roman laughs. "Ain't that the truth. Will the little cunt be there as well?"

My anger begins to boil, but I remind myself Xavier's playing a role.

"I have no doubt that she'll follow them wherever they go."

"Well, it sounds like a good plan, but why did you need to tell me down here? We'll still have to inform the others when they get here."

We don't hear Xavier respond, but we do hear a loud pop and a crash which causes me to jump. My hand flies to my mouth, and I continue to stare down at the phone. Please don't let anything have happened to Xavier.

"Chevelley," Xavier's voice comes over the line in a hushed tone. "He's out for now, you have ten minutes before people start showing up. Have Gage drive you as close as possible. Come around the back like you did once before, I'll meet you at the gate. Hurry up."

He hangs up before I can reply. My heart leaps in relief that he's alive, but it soon drops to the pit of my stomach at the realization that I'm about to sneak into Roman Rios' house and come face to face with him.

Gage is already speeding down the road.

"C, you better be careful. I don't like this."

"He's giving me what I wanted. To see Roman take his last breath."

"What if Roman comes to and kills you both? He now knows that Xavier is not on his side, and he's not gonna be happy."

"I don't have time to worry about that. I just know that I owe this to my father."

Gage pulls up alongside the same alley me and Jasper snuck down to peek over Roman's fence.

"We'll be out here keeping an eye on things," Silas says before I hop out of the truck.

"I know. I'll see you guys soon."

I scurry down the dark alley and soon I see Xavier push open the back gate. I run right into the backyard.

"This way, let's go," he demands.

He grabs my hand and pulls me along. When we get to the back door, Xavier steps inside and looks around first, before signaling me to follow him.

I hear voices somewhere in the house, but they don't sound too close. We speed walk through a large kitchen bathed in white. Everything is spotless, but the stark white walls and appliances make it seem clinical rather than homey.

We make a left turn and pass a dining room that holds a table that can sit at least twelve people. The house is huge, and I kind of feel like I'm in a maze. Xavier makes one turn after another until we reach a small door. He takes out a key to unlock it, and then we're descending a flight of stairs.

My heart picks up speed, because I know Roman's down here. I just don't know if he's conscious or not. Is he gonna be waiting for us? I don't know.

When my foot hits the last step, Xavier turns around. "He's tied up, don't worry."

I nod and breathe a sigh of relief. "What's the plan?" I whisper.

"Just follow my lead."

I follow Xavier further into the basement, but calling it a basement doesn't seem right. It's cloaked in white as well. White walls, white floors, and white containers everywhere. It's clean and well put together. There's a few furniture pieces on one side, and in one of the chairs is Roman. He's still unconscious, his head lolling to the right and his arms tied behind him.

"What did you do to him?" I ask.

"Hit him in the temple with my gun. He'll wake up soon," Xavier says, kicking at his chair.

"Are you just gonna kill him in here and then leave?"

"No."

Before I can ask what the plan is, Roman begins to stir. When he's finally able to focus, he looks at me first. His eyebrows furrow deeply, causing the wrinkles in his forehead to become more prominent. He tries moving, but he can't.

"What the fuck are you doing here, you little bitch?"

Roman snarls, spit shooting from his mouth. "And you," he growls, looking at Xavier, "you will fucking die for this. Did you forget my little insurance policy I have in order? You kill me, you kill her."

Xavier smiles a sardonic smile. "I've waited for this day for so many years. Did you think I'd really be okay with you killing my father? I've loathed you since the day I met you. It was because of you that I went to prison. It was because of you that I was left with nothing. You took my life away, but it's okay, because it led me to this moment."

"Shut the fuck up, you worthless piece of shit. If it wasn't for me, you'd be a bum on the street. I should've killed you when I killed your useless father."

In an instant, Xavier has a gun raised, a silencer on the end is aimed at Roman's knee, and then Roman's knee is no more. Blood goes everywhere, staining the white floor beneath us.

Roman cries out, his body jolting and moving the chair.

"I'd choose your words carefully," Xavier replies.

"Fuck off," Roman grunts through pain. "My men will find you. They'll make sure you watch as that little whore of yours gets her head cut off, just like her old man."

My stomach lurches, but I don't throw up. Instead, I grab the gun from Xavier and fire right at Roman's crotch. Blood seeps through his dark-colored pants.

"You son of a bitch," I sneer. "I'll make you suffer for what you did to my father."

I shoot him once more in the right foot, and then Xavier takes the gun away from me. Tears burn the back of my eyes, and bile rises in my throat. Not for what I'm doing to Roman, but because I believe him when he says what happened to my father. I try to shake the images from my head and focus on the task at hand.

Xavier walks over to the containers and begins uncovering them while Roman continues to cry out in pain. I watch him suffer and think to myself that he deserves so much worse.

I look around and notice all the containers now have their lids off, and Xavier is bringing forth a gas can. Roman's eyes widen in fear and he shakes his head profusely.

Xavier checks his watch. "Everybody should be upstairs already. It's ten minutes after your scheduled meeting time. Can you guess what's going to happen to you all?" He sticks the gun in the back of his pants, hands me the gas can, and lifts up one of the containers. "She and I are going to walk out of here, but I can't say that about the rest of you."

Roman begins calling out for help, but Xavier doesn't seem too concerned that anybody will hear him. He just turns his back and walks up the stairs, instructing me to pour out the gasoline the entire way.

When we approach the top, he makes sure nobody is outside the door before having me wait by the wall.

"Wait here. I have to take this near the room everybody's waiting in. It won't be long."

He takes the gas can from me and sets off across the room and towards the voices. A couple minutes later, he's back, pouring out the remainder of the gasoline.

"Be ready to run," he says, handing me a book of matches. "Strike it and throw it on the stairs." I nod. "As soon as you toss it, run that way, down the hall. I'll be right behind you."

I strike my match and hear him strike his. As soon as I toss mine, I see the flames ignite in a narrow path making their way down the stairs, and I run. Xavier throws his in the direction of his other gasoline path, and we're both running down the hall at full speed.

Xavier grabs my hand and makes all the necessary turns to get us out the house. Because of the running, it doesn't seem to take as long getting out as it did getting in.

Before we leave through the back door, I hear a rumble of confused voices.

"Hurry, we don't have long," Xavier announces.

We're at the gate when I hear a small boom.

"What the fuck was that?" I ask.

"Keep moving!" he says, pushing through the gate and into the alley.

I spot Gage's truck at the end of the entrance and start running even faster. Another loud boom fills the night, and then it sounds like extreme fireworks going off. I chance a look behind me and can already see flames and smoke billowing into the sky.

Xavier lifts me and tosses me into the back of the truck. Gage speeds off, but with the direction we're going, we get a perfect view of Roman's house. Some of the windows have blown out, and flames are bursting through. The entire thing is lit up, brightening up the end of the block.

I'm thankful Roman has a corner house, and the other house is too far away to be affected by the fire.

As much as we'd all love to sit and watch it burn to the ground, we know the police and fire department will be here soon, and we need to be far away.

"What was in those containers?" I ask Xavier as we fly down the street.

"Explosives. I found out that Roman's been ordering bomb making materials and he keeps them down there."

"So, there's no way he could have survived."

He shakes his head. "No."

We stay silent the rest of the trip, but he keeps his arms around me, trying to keep me warm. I try not to think of what happened to my father, but I can't help it, and a few tears trickle down my cheeks. I attempt to swipe at them without bringing attention to them, but Xavier doesn't miss a thing. He wipes the tears with his thumb and gives me soft kiss on the forehead. I curl into him and weep into his shirt.

When we arrive back to my house, Xavier helps me out of the back of the truck and all four of us make our way into the living room.

It's a surreal feeling knowing the man we've all been wanting dead for so long is finally gone. It almost doesn't feel real, and I probably won't believe it until it's reported that there were no survivors.

"So, what happened in there?" Silas asks as we all sit down.

Xavier tells them what happened while I kind of sit in a trance. I can't believe he's dead. I can't believe this whole thing is finally over. All the bloodshed and lives lost finally comes to an end.

"Chevelley, you okay?" Gage asks, concern etched on his face.

"Yeah. It almost feels like it didn't happen. I just want confirmation. You know?"

"Oh, it happened," Silas says. "There's no way anybody was walking out of that house."

"I know." I get up from the couch and start walking towards the kitchen when Gage's phone rings.

"It's Rem," he says before answering.

I grab a bottle of vodka and a Sprite and mix them in a large glass. I get down my first gulp when Silas walks in behind me.

"Hey. You okay?"

I push a few loose strands of hair out of my face.

"Yeah, I'm fine. Is Gage telling Rem what happened?"

"Yeah. We'll make sure everybody knows soon."

I nod and take another drink. "Hey, what were you going to tell me about Xavier?" I ask quietly.

Silas steps back and looks into the living room, trying to see where X is. "Look, I don't know what's going on with you guys, or if anything will happen, but I don't think Xavier would ever tell you this, and you should know."

"Okay, well . . ." I say, gesturing with my hand for him to spit it out.

"When he first started working with Roman, he tried to get away. He was given the car for an errand and he took that opportunity to run. He made it back into town and even got here, to this house. He was just getting out of the car when a couple of Roman's guys came around the corner. Apparently, Roman had called ahead and had people waiting, because he knew this is where Xavier would come." Silas takes a breath and another peek into the living room before continuing. "They beat him, C. They took him back to Roman and he beat the shit out of him even more. He was treated like a dog, probably worse. Roman told him that if he ever got close to you again, he'd do the same things to you that he had already done to Xavier."

"Oh my God," I whisper, horrified.

"He's been through a lot, Chelle. And most of it has been because of you. Now, I don't mean that in a bad way. You had no idea, none of us did, but that guy tried coming back to you, and it cost him even more. He had to make sure you didn't want to be near him, because if Roman ever saw . . . well, you know."

My eyes begin to burn with tears fighting to come out. "Why? Why would he do all of that? Risk his life?"

Silas furrows his brows. "Why does anybody give up

part of themselves for someone? Why do people sacrifice and protect someone with all that they have?" He raises his brows like he's waiting for me to figure it out.

"You think he . . ." I trail off, unable to say the word he and I never spoke to each other.

"I do."

I take another drink and Silas squeezes my shoulder and walks off. I continue to stand there with my drink in my hand until footsteps behind me grab my attention.

When I turn, I'm face to face with Xavier. He looks me up and down.

"Can I have a taste?" he asks with a glint in his eye and smirk on his lips.

I put a hand on my hip. "I don't know. Will I be in trouble for giving you some?" I ask with a grin, remembering the night we first spoke so many years ago.

The double entendre sits heavy between us.

"You have no idea," he says in a low purr. "But you love trouble."

He steps up to me and wraps his hand around mine on the glass and brings it to his mouth. His eyes never leave mine while he drinks.

"Mm," he moans, licking his lips. "I haven't tasted *that* in so long."

My lips part and I inhale sharply, but quietly.

"Oh?"

He studies my face, and then begins leaning in. His lips are so close to mine I can almost feel them.

And then I see Gage walk in.

"Hey. Oh. Uh," he stammers. "I just talked to everybody."

Xavier grins at me before coming around to stand next to me.

"Even Johnny and Lou? You know if you don't tell Johnny something again, he'll have your balls."

He makes a face. "I know. I told them, too."

Silas joins us. "This shit is fucking over. Thank fucking God!"

"I need a fucking vacation," Gage says, rubbing the back of his neck.

"Oh, that would be nice! All of us should go somewhere. I'm sure Rem, Trax, and Deacon would be on board, and of course I'd have to invite Lee, because I need someone to talk about you guys to," I say with a wink.

"X, you down?" Silas asks.

"Well, I don't have a job to worry about," he quips.

"Hey, man," Gage says, looking at X. "I'm sorry I didn't believe you right away, but I know you know why. I'm glad to have you around again, though."

Xavier nods. "I do understand." He looks down at me. "I'm glad to be around again."

"Alright, well, I'm going to bed," Silas announces. "Let's get the other guys over soon and have a celebration of sorts. We can figure out vacation details then. Johnny and Lou will be here to take care of any business that may arrive while we're gone."

"Okay," I respond. "I'll grab some food tomorrow."

Gage and Silas leave the kitchen, leaving Xavier and I alone again.

"You tired?" Xavier asks when he sees me trying to stifle a yawn.

"A little."

"Well, do you mind if I stay over? I don't have my car here. It's parked a couple blocks away from Roman's."

"Oh, shit. I forgot about your car. Yeah, of course you can stay. I'll take you to your car tomorrow. Umm. You want to stay in my room?"

I don't know why I feel so nervous asking him that, but my stomach flip flops waiting for his answer.

"If that's where you want me."

"Well, we do have a spare room, but I haven't had time to change the sheets and everything. It was Jasper's room."

"Don't worry about it then. Your room is fine. I'll even sleep on the floor if you want," he says with amusement in his voice.

I roll my eyes. "Whatever. Come on."

I'm sure to turn off all the lights downstairs before going to my room. Once Xavier closes the door behind us, my heartrate spikes.

"Well, uhh, the bed is a king, so we can both sleep comfortably in it. No need to sleep on the floor," I say, adjusting the covers and pillows.

He takes off his black jacket and throws it on the back of the chair that sits in the corner. I watch as he sits down and begins taking off his shoes, placing them neatly under the chair. He looks up and catches me staring at him. My cheeks feel hot, and I quickly turn around and start pulling things from the dresser.

"Can I use your shower?" he asks.

"Oh, yeah. Towels are in there," I reply, pointing towards the bathroom.

He grins at me, his smile telling me he knows how nervous I am.

While he showers, I sit on the bed and fidget. And then I'm up and pacing around the room. I send a text to Lee, but she doesn't answer. She's probably asleep.

Xavier emerges from the bathroom wearing only a pair of boxer-briefs. His body makes me stop in my tracks.

His physique is phenomenal, from his broad shoulders, perfect chest, and muscled arms to his unbelievably cut abs and thick, toned legs. His tanned skin still has a few droplets of water on it, and I want nothing more but to lick them off.

I note a handful of scars on his body, and I can't help but remember the beatings Roman and his guys gave him.

"All yours," he says.

"What?" I ask, finally looking up at his face. "What's all mine?"

He gives me another amused smile. "The bathroom."

"Oh. Yeah. Thanks."

I rush past him and lock myself in the bathroom. I think this shower will be a cold one. Holy fuck.

Once I'm out of the shower, I put on an extra-large shirt and a pair of cotton shorts. I tell myself I don't need to put anything sexy on. We're just sleeping.

I put my hair in a ballerina bun on the top of my head, brush my teeth, and head into the room. Once again, Xavier takes my breath away. He's lying on my bed, leaning against the headboard with his arm over his head. In his other hand, he holds the remote to the TV. He's flipping through the channels, the covers coming to a stop at his waist, allowing me a perfect view of his sculpted torso.

He looks so comfortable.

So at home.

I sigh and make it over to the bed.

"There's not really much on TV," he says.

"Never is."

I turn off the light, climb into the bed, and pull the covers over my body. He clicks off the television and puts the remote on the table next to him.

"Come," he says, and I turn to look in his direction.

It's taking a while for my eyes to adjust, but when I'm finally able to see him, I see he has his left arm stretched out.

I scoot over and lie my head on his chest. He wraps

his arm around my shoulders and brings his other arm around and places it on my waist.

"Goodnight, Chevelley," he says softly, kissing my forehead.

"Goodnight, Xavier," I reply.

# CHAPTER 21

WHEN I WAKE UP, I stretch my body out and find that Xavier is no longer in the bed. I open my eyes and look around the room, but he isn't in here. I slowly make my way out of the bed and into the bathroom.

Once I'm dressed and ready—this time with a tiny bit of makeup on—I go downstairs, following the sound of the TV.

"Hey, you're not sleeping your life away," Gage says when he sees me.

"Ha ha. Where's Si and X?"

"They went to the grocery store."

"How long have you all been awake?"

"An hour or so."

He turns his attention back to the TV and I go make some coffee.

"How does it feel? With Xavier being around?" I ask.

"It's a little strange, I'll admit. But, it's okay. We'll get reacquainted and be close again. It'll just take a little while."

"Yeah."

"How's things between you two?" he asks. "Are you guys . . ."

"No." I shake my head. "We haven't done anything. Nothing's official. We're still figuring stuff out, I guess.

I don't know."

He nods and doesn't press the issue.

"So, are we having everybody over tonight?"

"Yep, but don't worry. We'll do the steaks and chicken on the grill. You can take care of the sides and whatever."

"Everybody coming?"

"Everybody but Johnny and Lou of course. They're too old to hang with us youngens," he says with a laugh. "Their words."

"I'll be sure to tell Lee."

"It'll be an interesting night. None of the other guys have been around Xavier since this whole thing came to light, so it'll be fun to see how they react."

I groan. "Oh, God, it's gonna be all awkward and tense, isn't it?"

He laughs. "Don't know."

By the time I finish my coffee, Silas and Xavier come in carrying several bags in each hand.

"Need help?" I ask.

"Nope," answers Silas.

Xavier smiles at me when he walks by and my insides turn to mush. Why does he have that effect on me?

Gage sees the dumb smile on my face and shakes his head, but a small grin touches his lips. I get up from the couch and find myself in the kitchen, helping them put everything away.

"You ready for tonight?" I ask Xavier.

"What's happening tonight?" he asks.

"Everybody's coming over for dinner."

"Oh," he says, like he wasn't expecting that to be what I was talking about. "Why wouldn't I be?"

"You know. They don't like you. Well, I mean . . . they didn't. They haven't been around you since, well, a long time ago."

"I'm not worried about those guys," he says. "Everything will be fine."

Always so confident.

"Did you want me to take you to your car still?"

"Oh yeah, I need to go to my house and change and take care of some things. Can you go now?"

"Yeah, sure."

A FEW MINUTES LATER, WE'RE driving down the road in my black Impala.

"Did you sleep well?" Xavier asks me.

I look at him briefly. "I did. Did you?"

"Yeah, it was a little strange, but I enjoyed it."

"Strange?" I ask, confused.

"I haven't slept in a bed that wasn't mine in a long time, and not with another person either. You take up a lot of space."

I glance at him and see he's watching me with a small smile. "Not *that* much space."

"You sleep like a starfish."

"A starfish?" I screech.

"Don't worry. A cute starfish."

"Oh my gosh," I say through my laughter.

A few minutes go by where neither of us say anything. I'm in my head thinking about the lack of sex that happened last night. I mean, with all the innuendos about tasting things, I figured he'd be the first to make a move. Maybe he was waiting to see what I did. As much as I'd like to say I want to take things slow, I want Xavier more. I want to feel his hands all over my body. I want to feel him inside of me. I want to hear is lust-filled grunts and moans. I squeeze my thighs together and try to shake the thoughts from my head.

"Take the right turn coming up," Xavier tells me. "I parked it just down here."

I follow his directions and pull up behind his car.

"So, I'll see you later then?"

"Yeah, I'll be there. Seven o'clock, right?"

"Yep."

He pauses with his hand on the door handle. "Chevelley, I didn't try anything last night because when I have you again, it's going to be a very long night with very loud noises. Something I wasn't comfortable doing with your roommates so close by." He grabs my hand and brings it to his mouth, kissing the back. "See you later."

"Yeah, later," I respond breathlessly.

AT SIX-THIRTY, I'M IN THE kitchen with Lee making some potato salad, deviled eggs, and a few other sides, including dessert. Gage, Silas, and Deacon are in the backyard getting the grill ready, but more than likely, just drinking beer.

"I can't believe I missed out on so much! I was on my deathbed for a few days. Stupid flu. So, Roman's gone and Xavier is back? Wow."

"The news reported today that there were no survivors at Roman's house, so we don't have to worry about him or any of his people coming after us again. It's a huge relief to be able to focus on our jobs without the threat of someone taking that away. And of course, without worrying about being killed."

"Well, of course," Lee scoffs, rolling her eyes. "Can't forget about the possibility of being killed."

I playfully elbow her. "Anyway, they don't have any suspects or anything, and I doubt they'll come looking for us. Roman had a lot of enemies."

"Well, that's good. I can't have you escaping death only to be put in jail."

"Oh!" I exclaim, just remembering the whole vacation thing. "We're going on vacation!"

"Who? You and Xavier?"

"What? No. All of us! You, too. You down?"

"Uh. Yeah," she says in her best valley girl voice. "Where we going?"

"We don't know yet."

"Hmm. Florida? California?"

"I don't know. We gotta make sure everybody agrees."

Lee scoops out the yolk of one boiled egg, putting it in a separate dish. "Xavier's going too?"

I cut into the potato. "Yeah. Silas actually asked him."

"Nice to see the boys are playing nice."

"Yeah."

I see her head turn and know she's staring me down. I ignore her and keep cutting the potatoes.

"You know you see me, Chevelley!"

"Huh? What's up?" I ask, not looking at her.

"What's going on with you and X? You guys gonna be staying in the same room when we go on vacation? You staying in the same room tonight? What the fuck?"

I laugh. "I don't know, Lee. He slept with me yesterday." She slams down her spoon and turns her whole body to look at me. "Not like that," I amend. "He didn't have his car here, and he actually slept in my bed."

"That's . . . weird."

"Well, he told me earlier that it was only because Gage and Silas were so close."

"Ah. I can understand that. Nobody needs to hear your sex noises."

"Shut up," I say, laughing.

"It's true. When you and Xavier get all serious, because you know it's gonna happen, you're gonna have to move in with him, or kick these guys out."

"Let's calm down on the moving in with people talk."

"You've loved that guy since you were a teenager. Just admit it."

"Anyway," I say, trying to get off the subject.

I finish the potato salad and cover it up. Lee's starting to scoop the deviled egg mixture back into the halved eggs.

"I'm not sure why you're trying to lie to me. You know I know. And, it's okay to love him now. Stop fighting it."

"We never said that to each other. I'm not about to say it a few days after finding out he actually isn't trying to kill me. It's too soon."

"Eight years is too soon? You loved him when you were eighteen! God, for someone so smart, you're being really dumb about this."

"You're lucky I love *you,* Lee," I say, giving her a stern look.

"I know," she chirps, giving me an exaggerated smile. "I'm just saying, even Silas knows there's love between you two. So, just say it. I love Xavier. You'll feel better once you say it out loud."

"When did you talk to Silas?" I ask, going to the fridge and pulling out the vanilla pudding.

"Earlier. Don't change the subject. Say you love Xavier. You know you want to."

I ignore her and begin pouring the pudding over the cut up pieces of pound cake. "This trifle is going to be delicious," I say, licking some of the pudding from my finger.

"Okay, one more time, and then I'm done with you. I love Xavier."

"You do?" Xavier's voice startles us both.

My head snaps in the direction of his voice. Lee's eyes are as wide as saucers, and she's yet to turn and face him. He's walking up behind her with amusement in his eyes.

"Oh, hey, Xavier," Lee says when she turns to look at him.

"I didn't know you loved me, Lee," he says with a charming smile.

"Uh. Well . . ." her eyes dart from me to him. "I just meant . . . you know. Someone else. I gotta go to the bathroom real quick. It's nice seeing you again."

"Uh-huh," he says, watching her dart out of the kitchen like she's being chased.

"You're early," I announce, hoping to move away from that awkward moment.

"I am. Gage was out front getting something from his truck and let me in. I wanted to say hi before I went out back."

"Oh."

I take in his outfit. The dark grey shirt he's wearing is molded to his body perfectly. He leans his hip against the counter, watching me place the sliced strawberries on top of the pudding.

"What're you making?"

"Strawberry trifle."

"Sounds good."

I smile. "It will be."

"Didn't know you were the regular Betty Crocker."

"I've lived with men my whole life. I've learned how to cook to keep them full and happy."

"They're pretty lucky, then," he says, picking up one of the whole strawberries and taking a bite. Now my eyes are drawn to his mouth. God, that mouth.

"I guess so."

"Well, I'm gonna step out back to have a smoke."

"Okay," I nod.

"Hey, Chevelley?"

"Hmm?"

"You're coming home with me tonight. Overnight. Okay?"

I takes a few seconds to register. I nod. "Yeah. Okay."

He smiles. "Good."

As soon as he's gone Lee comes bursting into the kitchen.

"Were you eavesdropping?" I ask.

"I was being polite and giving you privacy. But, yes, I heard everything. Tonight!" she screeches.

I shake my head, but can't help but laugh at her. "Tonight," I breathe.

"Are you nervous? Did you shave?"

"Yes and yes."

"He's even hotter than he used to be. Holy fuck, Chelle. How have you not taken advantage of him yet?"

"I don't think Xavier's a man you can take advantage of."

"True."

"Alright, well, hand me the whipped cream out of the fridge, so I can finish this off. Then, let's take a shot. I need to calm my nerves. Xavier gets me all . . ." I make my body shiver, because there aren't words to describe what he does to me.

"I get it," Lee says.

Right after we knock back a shot of whipped cream-flavored vodka, I hear voices at the front door. When I get into the living room, I see Rem and Trax making their way inside.

"Hey guys!" I greet.

"Hey, C."

"The guys are out back already. Smoking, drinking,

not cooking probably. Rem, can you whip 'em into shape for me?" I ask.

"You know I got it under control," he answers with a wink. "Where's our new friend?" he asks, looking around.

"Old friend," I correct. "He's with the guys out back."

"Oh, so he's one of the guys now, huh?" Trax asks.

"Both of you be nice."

"He's the one who shot us," Rem says with a laugh.

"Ugh. Just be good. Play nice. He'll be around more often now."

"You know I'm a nice guy, C," Trax says, making his way to the back door.

"He'll be around more often now, huh?" Rem repeats. "Does that mean I'm losing my piece of ass?"

I shove him in his good shoulder. "You're an ass, and yes, that's what that means, and if you want to not get shot again, I wouldn't say that around X."

"Yeah, yeah. Well, I'm happy for you. For us all, really. No more Roman. It feels good to walk down the street and not have to look over my shoulder every five seconds."

"I know. Did Gage tell you about vacation?"

"Who's going on vacation?"

"All of us. You wanna come, right?"

"Sure."

"We'll pick a place later. Come on, let's go make sure those guys are cooking."

When we get outside, Lee is standing in between Deac and Xavier, seemingly being a buffer. Gage and Silas are hovering around the grill, and Trax is sitting in one of the chairs sipping from a beer bottle.

"How's it goin' over here, guys?" I ask, walking towards the grill.

"Food should be done in about twenty minutes,"

Gage answers.

I watch as Rem walks towards Xavier. I bite down on my lip and find myself holding my breath. Please let this go over well.

"What're you lookin' at?" Silas asks before following my gaze. "Oh."

I watch Xavier stare down Rem as he approaches. They're just out of earshot, so I have no way of knowing what's being said. Xavier's face doesn't soften, and he doesn't smile, he's listening to whatever Rem has to say. Finally, he nods his head towards Rem's shoulder, saying something I can't quite hear. Rem glances down and shrugs. They're obviously talking about his injury, which considering the circumstances in which he got it, has to be uncomfortable.

They speak for a few more minutes and then Xavier says something that makes Rem break into laughter. He slaps Xavier on the back with a smile on his face and then calls Trax over. Whatever X said, broke the ice, and now Rem is going to make sure him and Trax mend their relationship.

I let out a huge sigh and feel like a hundred pounds was just taken off my shoulders. It may not be completely fixed yet, but we're taking the right steps to restore what we once had.

We all sit around the one table we have in our backyard, and wait for the food to be done. When it is, we make our way inside and gather around the dining room table. Each seat is full, food covers the table, and laughter fills the house.

I look around at all my friends—my family—and smile. I wish Jai, Jasper, and my dad were still here, but I couldn't be happier to have the people I have left surrounding me.

Everybody engages in different conversations around

the table, nobody being left out. The food goes quickly, most everyone getting seconds. When we're all done, and all the mess has been cleaned up, we linger between the kitchen and living room, enjoying some drinks.

Lee and Deac seem to be getting friendly, and I know it's only a matter of a time before that becomes official.

I'm standing at the sink washing my hands when someone brushes up against me. I freeze when I feel a large hand slowly make its way around the curve of my hip, coming to a rest on my stomach. Xavier's lips graze my ear, sending chills down the right side of my body.

"You almost ready to leave?" he whispers huskily.

He's so close that when I turn to look at him, our mouths are almost touching.

"Mm. Yeah, I'm ready. Let me just grab some things from my room."

"I'll be saying my good-byes," he says softly. He caresses the side of my neck with his hand, his thumb grazing my throat before it moves to my bottom lip. "I can't wait to get you alone," he growls before pressing his lips to mine briefly.

I'm left both speechless and breathless, and all I can do is watch him saunter off. I quickly rush through the living room and up the stairs, getting Lee's attention and telling her to follow me.

"I'm about to leave with Xavier. Are you gonna be okay here?"

She rolls her eyes. "You act like I don't know these guys. Of course I'll be fine."

"Okay," I say, gathering some clothes and toiletry items and throwing them in a duffle bag.

"I don't have to ask if you're gonna be okay," she says, waggling her eyebrows at me.

"I'll call you when I'm back home," I say, kissing her cheek and rushing past her.

"You better," she replies, following me down the stairs.

Xavier's standing at the door waiting for me. He reaches out for my bag. "I'll meet you in the car."

"Okay."

I find Gage in the kitchen. "Hey, I'm leaving. I'll be back tomorrow."

He turns and raises his brows. "Xavier?"

"Yep!" I say without apology.

"Well, okay then. Be careful."

"See you later," I say, stretching up onto my tip toes and kissing his cheek.

When I'm walking back through the living room, I announce my departure to everyone.

"I'm outta here, kids. I'll see you guys later."

A few of them look confused at first, and then realization hits. Rem smirks at me, Lee looks all giddy, and the others just lift a hand a wave.

"See ya," a couple voices reply.

And then I'm gone.

Xavier waits for me in his car, leaning over to open my door from the inside.

"Ready," I announce when I get in.

He grins. "Oh, Chevelley. You have no idea what I have in store for you."

# CHAPTER 22

WHEN WE WALK INTO XAVIER'S house, he drops my duffle bag on the floor and I'm instantly pushed against the wall in the entryway.

"I've been waiting for this for so long," he breathes against my mouth. "Years, Chevelley. For years I've been waiting to be close to you again. To feel your body against mine. To taste you. I can't wait any longer." His mouth runs along my neck, planting passionate kisses as his hands grip my waist.

"Don't wait anymore," I say softly.

With that, I'm lifted up, my legs wrapped around him as he carries me upstairs. Xavier places me on the bed, and strips the clothes from my body. He does this slowly and methodically, driving me insane in the process. My socks and shoes go first, and then he dips his fingers into the waistband of my shorts, popping open the button and dragging them down my legs.

As he brings them down, he kisses a path across my thighs, nibbling at the innermost part. I gasp and my back arches off the bed.

He comes back up and leisurely pushes my shirt up, licking my stomach in the process. Once he's taken it off completely, he focuses his attention on my breasts. They're encased in a black lace bra, pushed up and together perfectly.

Xavier kisses the tops of them softly, switching back and forth while maneuvering his hands behind me, unhooking the clasps. He tosses the material to the side and his mouth covers my right nipple and he begins to suck. I grip the covers in my hands, my body squirms beneath him, begging for more.

He doesn't ignore a single section of my body. His mouth reacquaints itself with every part of me, and my body thoroughly enjoys the reunion.

By the time he moves in between my legs, I feel like I might explode. My black panties are still on, and his tongue snakes out, licking the length of me through the material. I hiss, squeezing my eyes closed and plead for more.

I feel his hands spread my legs further apart, and he teases me mercilessly as he kisses, licks, and nibbles on my inner thighs and then my bikini line, and finally, all the way up to the top of my panties. He pays attention to every area except the one I'm wanting him to the most. His fingernails lightly graze the sides of my legs as he once again presses his flattened tongue on my clit through the material. I feel the wetness and warmth, but it's not enough.

"Xavier, please!" I beg.

Without words, he pulls my panties off, and I'm sure my pussy is glistening before him.

He groans before he lowers his face once again. The tip of his tongue runs up the length of me, and he continues that motion, giving me more of his tongue each time. After a while, his tongue is flattened, massaging my clit over and over.

"Oh, God," I moan, my body near convulsions as I tighten my grip in his hair. "Yes, yes," I chant.

With my clit being so engorged and sensitive, each

stroke of his tongue sends me even closer to the edge of bliss. I feel my body tightening up, and my moans and chants come faster and louder until I feel one finger slide inside me while his tongue flicks my most sensitive area.

Then, I'm free-falling into a blissful world where nothing else exists except the sheer pleasure of what Xavier gave to me. I cry out loudly, pulling at his hair and curling my toes.

"Jesus Christ," I pant after I come down from the waves of orgasm.

Xavier takes the time to remove his clothes, giving me my own personal strip show. He grabs a condom from his nightstand, rips it open, and sheaths his impressive cock.

He grabs my ankles and pulls me closer to him. Hovering over my body with his face near my neck, he thrusts in hard and fast, filling me completely.

I yell out in surprise.

"Fuck," he growls, his voice full of rasp.

He holds himself over me, giving me long and deep strokes. My nails dig into the back of his shoulders and make a trail all the way to the top of his ass. Xavier fucks me hard, sending my body further up the bed.

He pulls out and flips me over, pulling me up by my waist until my ass is in the air with my chest pressed against the mattress. His rough hands grab ahold of my hips as he slides his thick cock into me slowly. Once he's buried to the hilt, he pulls almost all the way out and then thrusts in fast and deep, eliciting a guttural yell from me.

I push my face into the pillow, grunting into the soft fabric as he works my body from behind. His hands squeeze my ass cheeks, giving me sporadic slaps before finding their home on my waist and squeezing while he drives in hard and fast.

An unbelievably intense feeling comes over me. It almost feels like an overwhelming urge to pee, but I know it's not that. He's hitting my g-spot with perfect precision. Thrust after thrust hits that spot, and he tops it off by reaching around and rubbing my clit with his fingers. With both places being stimulated, I feel almost out of control of my body. It shakes, and then it tightens up. I grind myself on him, and then I stop and let him do the work. A few minutes later, that ethereal feeling comes back, but even stronger.

I can feel it building, and building, and building until it reaches max intensity and then I explode.

I scream so loud, my throat instantly becomes raw. The orgasm seems never ending and I can feel an insane amount of wetness between us. His thrusts never slow, but he does take control of my hips with both hands again and plunges into me over and over.

He grunts, his grip becoming tighter, and his thrusts gaining speed. When he releases, he lets out a raspy roar, and collapses on my back.

Once he's caught his breath, he pulls out and I drop down onto my stomach, my body unable to keep me up any longer.

He tosses the condom and comes back to join me on the bed. Our naked limbs become entangled, and even though I still feel overheated, I can't bring myself to move away from his body.

"Mmm," I moan, fully sated.

"Mmhmm," he moans, sounding just as pleasured as I do.

"That's only round one. We have plenty more catching up to do," he says.

"How many rounds do you think you can last?" I ask playfully.

"As many as it takes."

"Takes to do what?"

"To convince you that I'm the only one who can take care of your body's needs."

After a brief pause, I say, "Count me convinced."

He looks down at me with a small amount of surprise on his face and then he smiles and leans in for a kiss.

We end up going another couple rounds before we both fall asleep, but in the time between rounds, we reminisce about our time together before. We joke, we laugh, and we snack on junk food.

I love this man. Irrevocably. Without apology. And with all that I have.

We've been through hell and back, but we've fought and clawed our way through that hell and made it out. I can't go without him again. I don't think I'll be able to handle it. Whether he knows it or not, he's stuck with me, because there's no way I'm letting him go again.

WHEN I WAKE UP, I wake up to the smell of coffee and bacon. As I walk to the bathroom to take a quick shower, I find my legs are sore like I ran a marathon last night. Actually, what happened last night was probably more energy exerting than running a marathon. I smile at the memory.

After my shower, I dab on some light makeup, and wrangle my wet hair into a braid, and then wrap it in bun. It'll give me some curls later once it's dry. I find my duffle bag on the floor by the closet and pull out a white, scoop neck t-shirt and black pants, and put them on.

Downstairs, I find Xavier sitting at the table reading the paper with a cup of coffee in front of him. He looks up when he hears me and smiles.

"Good morning. I made some bacon and eggs, if you're hungry."

"Starved. Thanks. Have you ate?"

"No. Just the coffee."

I make us both a plate and sit next to him at the table. He folds and places the paper next to him, and takes my hand. "It's nice to have you here."

I smile. "It's nice being here."

The entire time we're eating our breakfast, I'm going over what I want to tell him. I have to get it out or it will eat at me. He seems to see the wheels turning in my head, because he moves the dishes to the kitchen and comes back, leading me to the couch.

"What're you thinking about?" he asks.

I give him a small grin. "A lot. Are you sure you're ready?"

"As ready as I'll ever be."

"Okay." I take a deep breath. "I know we've been through a hell of a lot. There was a long period of time where I was sure we'd never be friends, never be anything but enemies. Up until this war with Roman started it was like we were strangers. We barely saw each other, there was no communication, and I had done my best to put you out of my mind. But now . . ." I trail off, trying to find the right words.

"But now?" he encourages, looking deep into my eyes.

"But now I want you to always be around. I want you in my life. We lost too many years, but we still have a connection. We never made things official before, choosing to not put a label on us, and refusing to acknowledge how we really felt, but I don't want to keep doing that."

"Chevelley, we can call this whatever you want to call it, but you never had to worry. I was and still am devoted to you, to making you happy, to keeping you with me. I've lost enough to last a lifetime, and I'll be damned if I lose you again. If you want the boyfriend-girlfriend label, that's fine, but we're so much more than that."

A huge grin stretches across my face. "Yeah?"

"Yeah, baby."

With that single term of endearment, my heart flutters and my stomach does a little flip. I crawl onto his lap, throw my arms around his neck, and kiss him passionately.

When we pull apart, he cups my face in his hands, studying me intently. "I love you, Chevelley. I always have and always will. When you gave yourself to me so many years ago, you owned me. I was always yours, just like you've always been mine. You can feel my love for you, right?"

I feel the tears making their way to the front of my eyes, the drops resting heavily on my lower lashes before cascading onto my cheeks.

I nod my head. "I love you, Xavier." He squeezes me as I bury my face into the side of his neck. "It feels so good to finally say it," I say in a half laugh, half sob sort of way.

"We always knew it was there, whether it was said aloud or not. We felt it."

I nod into his neck, and we stay in that tight embrace for a couple minutes. When we break apart, it's because Xavier lays me down on my back across the couch cushions.

"I'm going to make sure you really feel my love for you," he says with a grin. "Your body will be able to feel every single inch of my love."

"Mmm," I moan in anticipation. "Let me feel it."

And I do. I feel all of it. Every. Single. Inch.

# CHAPTER 23

*Six weeks later*

IT'S BEEN SIX WEEKS SINCE Xavier and I finally told each other how we felt. Six weeks of countless I love yous, off the charts sex sessions, date nights, sleepovers, and lots of talking.

Nobody was surprised when I announced that Xavier and I were in a relationship. The guys have come full circle and accepted Xavier back into our group. There's no hatred and no rivalry, everybody gets along.

Lee has finally submitted to Deacon-as he likes to say. They spend almost as much time together as Xavier and me.

Roman's house going up in flames remains a mystery to the cops, and that's how we want it. Our business has been able to function like normal again, us doing what we've always done, looking out for the best interest of our clients. There was some tension between one of our clients and one of his enemies who seems dead set on fucking with his club, and we've had to put in some work there. The strip club also functions as a money laundering facility; dirty money goes in, clean money comes out, but that's not our business, we just make sure nobody fucks with it.

Not only is Xavier part of our group as a friend, he's also working with us. However, he and I have discussed branching out into something else. Something legit. We want to create a place for teenage youth who have lost a parent or both parents, to be able to go to not only get counseling, but find friends, mentors, and a place to go that feels warm and inviting. A place that feels like home.

It's still in the beginning stages, but we want the building to house counselors for the teens, a rec room for them to hang out in with other kids, and a gym for playing basketball, volleyball, and any other indoor sport.

I want to have parties for every holiday, bringing in food and drinks for the teens and their families. It would basically be a giant home with a ton of people always around, always willing to help, or just to listen.

I have no doubt that we'll make this dream happen, because it means a lot to both of us.

"Alright, everybody!" Gage hollers from the dining room. "Come in here."

He's invited everybody over, telling us he has some sort of announcement to make.

"Alright, what's up?" I ask.

"Two things. The first thing is we still have to figure out this vacation shit. I know things got a little busier than we planned with work, but in about two weeks, we'll finally have the time to get outta here for a while. So, let's all take a vote on where we want to go. Anybody want to go to Florida?" he asks.

"Ooh! I wouldn't mind Florida," Lee chirps.

"I'm down for whatever," Deacon adds.

"What about California?" Gage questions.

"Could we go to Disney?" Lee asks.

The guys all groan.

"You guys suck," she pouts.

"What about Vegas?" Rem chimes in.

"Oh my gosh, yes!" Lee says, jumping up and down. "Why didn't we think of that?"

"I think Vegas would be perfect. It's like Disneyland for adults," I say. "Guys?"

"Fuck yeah. I've never been before," Silas says.

"Well, if everybody's good with that, Vegas it is."

"Chevelley, we have got to start looking up all the places we can go!" Lee exclaims. "I'm gonna grab my phone."

She and Deacon walk off, and Trax and Rem go into the kitchen talking about strip clubs in Vegas.

"Hey, C, I want to tell you something else," Gage says.

"What's up?"

He looks at Silas and then back at me and Xavier. "Well, Silas and I have been thinking about it a while, but don't take it the wrong way. We've decided to move out. Both of us have found places to live that aren't too far away. We moved in here when we were younger, Memphis taking us in when we had no other option. We'll always be grateful, but now that you and X are serious and spending more time together, we only thought it was right to give you guys space."

I feel a little sad at their announcement, but I always knew it was going to happen eventually. "Well, I guess I can't say I'm too surprised. I mean, you guys are old as shit," I say jokingly. "Seriously, though, I am going to miss you guys being around all the time. I love you both so much, but I understand the need to have your own place."

"We'll miss you, too, but we'll still be around all the time," Silas says, coming around to hug me.

When they walk off, Xavier sits down in the chair

next to me.

"You okay?" he asks.

"Yeah, I'll be fine. I always knew they weren't going to live here forever. It's just gonna take some getting used to. I've never lived alone."

"Do you want to?"

I shrug. "It's such a big house for one person, but I can't bring myself to sell it. It's my father's house. You know?"

He nods, seemingly in thought about something. "Do you want to live with me, Chevelley?" he asks, shocking me completely. "I know you just said you didn't want to sell this place, but if you're okay with it, I can move in here. I had planned on asking if you wanted to live together, anyway, and now seems as good a time as any."

"Are you serious?" I ask, my eyes going wide.

"I'm serious about us."

"Yes! Yes, I'd love that, Xavier. The back and forth sleepovers was getting old anyway," I say with a laugh.

He seems to breathe a sigh of relief, like he was actually worried I would say no. We hug, and I can't wipe the smile from my face. Lee walks over with a curious look on her face.

"What's going on over here?" she asks in a sing-song voice.

"We're moving in together!" I almost yell.

"Aaah!" she squeals, clapping her hands. "I'm so happy for you guys. Who's going where? What about . . ." she jerks her head towards Silas and Gage.

"They already found places to live. We're gonna live here," I say with a smile.

"Well, it's all worked out, then. That's great. Now, come look at Las Vegas stuff with me."

We both laugh, and I let her pull me to the living room. Xavier joins up with the other guys and he must tell them the news, because I see them slapping him on the back and shoulder with smiles on their faces.

Later that night, we all book our plane tickets and reserve our hotel rooms in Las Vegas. Sin City, here we come.

# EPILOGUE

*Two weeks later*

WE FLY INTO LAS VEGAS around sundown. The Strip is already lit up, but the sun still peeks out over the horizon. Lee and I shove our faces into the windows, oohing and ahhing at the sights below us.

In the two weeks we had to wait to fly out, Silas and Gage moved out, and Xavier moved in. Everybody pitched in and helped move all of Silas' and Gage's furniture out of my house and into their new ones, and helped move Xavier's stuff into *our* house. Between what I had and Xavier's furniture, we were able to give them both a few living room furniture pieces and dining room pieces. Xavier brought over everything he had, so we just made it to where we didn't have double.

"So, what are we doing first?" Lee asks with excitement.

"First, we have to get our rental cars and find the hotel," Gage says. "And, I don't know about you guys, but I'm fucking hungry, so we need to find food ASAP."

As soon as we get our luggage, we make our way through the airport looking for the company we reserved rental cars from. Both Lee and I are excited to see that they have slot machines in the airport.

"Hold on, hold on," Lee says, digging into her purse. "Let me play one of these real quick."

Gage huffs. "Go on ahead," I tell him. "We'll catch up."

All of the guys except Xavier and Deacon keep walking. Lee and I play a few times, but don't win a dime.

"If this is indicative of what it's gonna be like here, I'm staying away from the slot machines," I say.

The four of us—who have become quite the foursome with double dates and dinner at our place—meet up with the rest of the group just as Gage gets his keys. Xavier steps up to grab his, since one of the cars is under his name.

"Win any money?" Gage asks.

"I don't want to talk about it," Lee pouts.

In the car, we maneuver through traffic, and I take a thousand pictures on my phone in the matter of minutes. Most are blurry, but I'm hopeful I got a few good ones.

"You know we'll be out there walking around, and you can take them then," Xavier says, squeezing my thigh and giving me a grin.

"Just pay attention to the road and don't worry about me."

I snap a few more.

"There it is!" Lee cries from the backseat, spotting the Luxor. "What's that bright light shining out of the top?"

"I don't know what it's for, but I heard it's the brightest light beam in the world," I answer.

Once we find parking—which takes entirely too long—we unload our luggage and check in. Xavier and I have our own room with Deacon and Lee sharing one a few doors down. The rest of the guys have separate rooms, but we're all relatively close.

"Okay, let's go freshen up, put our shit away, and then meet up and find somewhere to eat. I'm sure they have a place in here," I say, looking around the pyramid shaped building.

Fifteen minutes later, we're all off in search of somewhere to eat. The casino floor is loud, the sounds of slot machines, cheering, laughing, and the occasional curse when someone loses money fill the area.

Luckily, we come across a burger place, because Gage was starting to get a case of the grumps caused by hunger.

The food is spectacular and we vow to come back before we have to leave. Everybody splits up after dinner, choosing to stay in the hotel and gamble and drink here. Tomorrow will begin our night of walking The Strip and finding clubs and other things to do. Everybody's starting to feel the effects of traveling, so I imagine it won't be a late night for any of us.

Xavier and I try our hand at blackjack first. I win a few times, but he wins a few more. I curse the slot machines after only winning a whopping one dollar and forty-seven cents when I put in a total of fifteen dollars. I knew I shouldn't have tried them again. Xavier wants to try craps, but I hold on to my chips, because I haven't a single clue how that game is played.

I venture to a table nearby that holds roulette. Seems simple enough. Place a bet, pick a color and number. Win or lose.

It's not that simple. Turns out there are more ways to bet than on a single number/color combo, so I walk back to Xavier. We leave the table a few minutes later with a handful more chips than we came with.

An hour later, we make our way to the room, ready for the comfort of a bed.

"SO, I WANT TO GO to the Stratosphere, the Bellagio, Paris, New York New York, and . . ." Lee looks down at some map of The Strip, "the MGM."

And that's exactly what we do. We take numerous breaks, because holy hell that's a lot of walking. After eating at some buffet in one of the hotels, we decide to head back to our hotel early before a night of clubbing.

I'm slipping on a form-fitting black dress with a sheer back when Xavier walks in.

"Oh my," he croons. "I'm not sure about this dress. I'd hate to have to kill somebody tonight."

"Very funny," I say, rolling my eyes. "Lee insists on dressing up. She says we won't be allowed in the clubs with jeans and tennis shoes on. You look very dapper Mr. Delgado," I say, admiring his black slacks and black button up.

"Why, thank you, Ms. Reed," he replies with a grin, pulling me against him. "I'm not gonna be able to keep my hands off of you tonight."

"Good," I murmur against his lips. "I like your hands on me."

I walk over to my bag and find the only heels I brought with me; black, patent leather pumps.

"I hope we aren't going to be walking a lot, because I have a feeling I'll have to carry you after a while if you're wearing those," he says, gesturing to my shoes.

"Hell no. I told Lee we will be cabbing it up tonight."

Someone knocks on our door, and Xavier goes to open it while I put on my shoes and check my makeup. Smokey eye, check. Nude lips, check. Curled hair that will most likely end up in a ponytail before the end of the night, check.

Lee whistles at me when she walks in the room. "You are smokin' hot! God, I want your boobs."

"You want the back aches to go with them?" I ask with a laugh.

"No, you can keep those."

"I thought so. You look good. I love that color on you," I tell her.

"Pretty in pink," she says twirling around. "That's

what the label says anyway."

"Well, in your case, it's true."

Her blonde hair is super straight and now ends just at the tops of her shoulders. She cut it before we came, wanting a fresh look.

"Mr. X looks mighty fine in there," she says, jerking her thumb behind her.

"If I didn't know better, I'd think you really did love me, Lee," Xavier says, walking into the room.

"You know. I'm just gonna stop talking," she says, trying to hide her embarrassment.

"Don't worry. I won't tell Deac," he says with a charming smile.

She rolls her eyes. "Deacon looks good, too. Wait till you see him, C! I picked out his outfit."

"I was just coming to get my wallet," Xavier says, kissing my cheek. "You ladies ready?"

"Yep," we answer together.

When we leave the room, everybody is standing outside the door waiting for us.

"Wow, you guys clean up nice," I say.

Silas and Gage both trimmed their beards. They're still pretty full and thick, but they look much neater than before. Each guy is wearing a different colored button up. Deacon has on a light blue that really makes his eyes standout. With the way his tattoos peek out over his collar, he looks like an inked model in a magazine spread. Lee was right, he does look good.

Gage went with a navy blue shirt, Silas a hunter green color. Rem looks good wearing a crisp, white shirt with black buttons. I really hope nothing gets spilled on him tonight, and Trax has on a nice grey shirt.

"Where to first?" Rem asks. "Strip club?"

Lee makes a scoffing noise. "No. We're going to a couple regular clubs first, and then we can talk about strip clubs. There's one in MGM that's five stories. Oh, and I saw a flyer for one called Club Trinity. It has three floors, obviously, and it seems to be really popular."

After some discussion, we decide on going to Club Trinity first.

We end up waiting outside for a good ten minutes before a couple cabs become available. The drive to Club Trinity doesn't take too long, but the traffic makes it seem further than it is. In all honesty, we could have walked, but I knew I'd be on my feet the entire time in the club, I didn't want to break out in blisters on the way.

"Wow, this place is awesome," Lee says in awe as we make our way inside.

"I can't wait to check out the other floors," I announce.

The first level has a very elegant feel. Cream colored couches with dark red pillows line two of the walls. Smaller tables along the other wall are pushed back into their own little alcoves, giving the people sitting there more privacy. Small chandeliers dangle above the tables, creating a dim, romantic light.

Lee drags Deacon onto the dance floor in the middle of the room while I find a table and Xavier goes off to order drinks. Rem and Silas go upstairs to the second level, while Trax and Gage check out the top level.

Half an hour later, the four of us on the first level go and search for the rest of the crew. The second club has a totally different feel. The room glows red with curved booths, black tables, and mirrors along one wall. The dance floor is broken into three pieces, all of which are set up higher than the main floor.

I spot the bar on the opposite end, and me and Lee go and order a tray of shots while Deacon and Xavier look for Rem and Silas.

"I really like this place," I tell Lee as we wait for the bartender. "I like that there's different music on each level and each portion has a completely different tone."

"I know. After we spend some time here, I wanna go upstairs and see what that one's like. Then we can go off to the MGM or wherever."

Lee orders eight shots. Two for both of us and two for our guys.

"Let's take one now. I'm not feeling any buzz yet," she says, forcing a shot glass into my hand.

We throw back the shot and Lee lets out a whooping sound. A girl next to us who seems to be enjoying her own shots turns around and whoops with her.

"Yeah, Vegas!" Lee yells.

"Whoo! Vegas!" The other girl shouts.

Her friend laughs. "Em, you live here."

"I don't care. Vegas is fucking awesome. Another shot!" she yells at the bartender.

Lee and I laugh, and her friend peeks around, shaking her head. "Sorry, she's drunk already."

Lee smiles. "Good for her! That's what we need to be."

"Well, let's take our second shot now," I say, grabbing another glass.

We swallow down the vodka and push the glasses back towards the bartender.

"Alright, let's get back to the guys," Lee says. "Rem's gonna want to go to a strip club soon, and I want to get more partying in before then."

"Hey, we know of a place you can go," one of the girls next to us says. "Sorry, I couldn't help but overhear. My fiancé's friend just opened up a new place. It's further away from The Strip, but it has a strip club, a regular night club, a quiet bar, and . . . some more interesting things. Something for you all to enjoy."

Her friend spins around on the stool.

"Full disclosure. Our guys own this place, so obviously we think you should stay here as long as possible, but the other guy who co-owns it with them opened this other place with a couple other people." She pauses to take a sip of her drink. "Anyway, back to the full disclosure thing. It's a huge estate, but it's a fetish club."

My eyes widen and I hear Lee gasp.

"Fetish like . . ." Lee starts to ask.

"It's not trashy. It's very upscale. Members only, but you can buy a one night membership card to try it out. It has a strip club, a nightclub, a lounge, and some other areas for sexual stuff, but you don't have to do that. We go all the time just because it's really nice and it's not as crowded as places down here. We're just here waiting for our guys to be done with some business so we can go over there."

"Kinky. Interesting," Lee says, looking at me with raised brows.

"I'm not sure if the guys will be on board," I say.

"There's a strip club! Of course they will be."

"Escorts too," the girl says. "Both male and female if you're interested. It's called The Cell if you want to look into it."

"Wow," I breathe. "Definitely unique."

"We'll try to convince our group," Lee says, grabbing two of the shots while I grab the others.

"If you end up going, just tell the guy at the front that Adrienne and Emilie invited you. It'll be fine. You're on vacation, right? You might as well enjoy it, because soon you'll have to go back to your mundane life back home."

Lee smirks and looks at me. "Yeah. Mundane describes your life pretty well."

I roll my eyes. "Thank you. Maybe we'll see you later."

"People in Vegas are friendly," Lee says as we walk away.

"People in Vegas are drunk," I add with a laugh.

We take our drinks back to where we left Xavier and Deacon and find the rest of the group there as well. We tell them about the girls we met and about the place they told us about. The guys suggest waiting until tomorrow night, just so we spread out things to do while we're here for the week.

We end up staying at Club Trinity the entire time, because a couple of the guys met some girls they wanted to keep talking to, and honestly, it was just a good time.

When we finally get back to the hotel at four in the morning after having one of the best nights of our lives, I flop onto the bed without bothering to take my dress off. However, the shoes were kicked off immediately.

"I'm so tired," I groan.

I feel the bed dip as Xavier straddles my thighs, unzipping my dress very slowly.

"Let's get you comfortable," he says seductively.

I turn over, allowing him to pull the dress off of me. I lie on the bed in my underwear and watch as he puts my dress on a chair near the window. He strips himself of his shirt and pants, placing them on the same chair before sauntering back over to me.

"Whatcha doing, Mr. Delgado?" I ask playfully.

"Getting comfortable," he says with a grin.

"Comfortable looks good on you."

He laughs, coming around to the bed and pulling the covers back. I crawl underneath them, making room for him to lay next to me.

"I know we've only been here for two days, but it's gonna be hard leaving here and going back home. Back to reality. Back to the same old shit."

"I have an idea," he says, turning on his side to face

me.

"What's that?"

"Why don't we think of it like going towards our future? Sure, we're going back to Philly, but we're moving towards our future. We've already taken the step to live together. We have that to look forward to."

I smile at him. "That's true."

"And we can really begin looking into creating that place for the teens."

"Yes, and we need to come up with a name for it as well."

"How about Delgado House?"

I furrow my brows. "But. .what about me? What about my name?"

He grins. "What if your name was Delgado?"

It takes me a few seconds to react. "What?" I say through nervous laughter.

"You heard me. We belong together, Chevelley. You are mine and I am yours. Nothing will keep us apart again. Our love survived lies, deceit, and bloodshed, but all's fair in love and war, and everything that was done was done in an effort to keep you in my life. There's no way that was for nothing. There's no way I'm living without you. So, will you be my wife?"

"Yes! Yes, of course. I love you so much, Xavier," I say, kissing his face and holding him tight.

"I love you, too," he says, capturing my mouth for a passionate kiss.

When we pull apart, I gasp, coming up with an idea. "Should we get married here? Everybody is already here. It would be perfect."

"Sounds like a perfect plan to me. We can do it right before we leave, giving us enough time to get our rings and your dress."

I lean in and kiss him again before pulling away and

getting up from the bed. Xavier watches me with curious eyes. I slowly unhook my bra, dropping it to the floor. My panties join it a few seconds later.

"What are you up to?" Xavier asks, his voice a low rasp.

I turn around and walk seductively towards the ice bucket and grab the bottle of champagne that came with the room. I take my time opening it, and pour two glasses. Xavier never moves his intense gaze from my naked body.

When I walk back with the glasses, I go to his side of the bed and come to a stop near his head, giving him a perfect view.

"We need to celebrate," I say, handing him a glass.

His eyes are glued to my pussy, and instead of reaching for the glass, he reaches for me.

"Uh-uh," I scold, taking a step back. "Let's toast first."

He growls, looking up into my eyes. "You aren't playing very fair, Ms. Reed."

I smile at him and hand him his glass. "Soon to be Mrs. Delgado, and you of all people know that all's fair in love and war."

He sits up and gulps down the champagne before tossing the empty glass behind him. I'm barely swallowing my first sip when he tosses my glass to the side and then tosses me onto the bed. I let out a high pitch squeal before he pounces on top of me with lust in his eyes.

"Hold on, baby, because you're in for one hell of a ride, and this one lasts a lifetime."

I smile and we celebrate our engagement until the sun comes up.

**THE END**

# A NOTE FROM THE AUTHOR

Dear readers,

Thank you so much for purchasing my book, I truly hope you enjoyed it. I had such a good time writing these characters. It's my first foray into the violent, criminal world, and I must say that I enjoyed it. If you did too, please leave a review.

To my escort series fans, that little part in the epilogue was just for you! I hope you enjoyed. To anybody who hasn't read The Escort Series, Em and Adrienne are from that series. The Cell is a place that is talked about in the end of book three. If you're interested in finding out more about those girls, their guys, friends, and experiences, pick up The Escort Series today.

Stay tuned for more from me, because I already have another book in the works.

Always,
Isabel

# ACKNOWLEDGMENTS

TO MY HUSBAND, THE LOVE of my life, my best friend, and my other half—I love you. Thank you so much for your support, your help, your ear when I need to ramble, your advice when I need it, your encouragement when I'm feeling down, and for just knowing exactly what I need when I need it. I couldn't get much done without you, and I'm so grateful to have you in my life. With you, I have everything I could ever need.

Tonya and Kizzy, my first beta readers, you both already know how much I love and appreciate you. I know I can count on you two for anything, and I'm forever thankful to have you both in my life. Thanks for your support, for the encouraging messages, for the laughs, for the help, but more importantly, for your friendship.

A quick shout out to my other girls who are forever tagging me in posts, pimping my books and teasers to blogs, and always willing to help me out. Iris, Beverly, Lupita, Traci, Lyndsey, Lindsay, Christina, and Felicia.

Thanks to Riza and Luisa for beta reading this one for me and giving me your opinions and thoughts on the story. You were both so fast getting back to me, and your feedback really helped. Thank you!

Yolanda Ann, you're awesome! I appreciate you always thinking about me when it comes to events or any sort of promotion.

To Kaprii, thank you for offering your help on my blitz and tour for WAR. I know it became a little hectic, but I appreciate the work you put into it.

Kylie from Give Me Books, thank you so much for putting together my release blitz, boost, and release party. Thanks for always responding so quickly to all of my messages and for all of the work you put into setting everything up.

Christine, thank you for your amazing skills when it comes to formatting. You are a genius, and you make my interior beautiful. I know when I hand over my baby to you, it's in good hands.

Robin, also known as The Best Cover Designer in the World! What else can I say that I haven't said already? Thank you a million times over. Each time I give you some ideas and pictures, you astonish me with what you come up with. I couldn't imagine working with anybody else. Thank you so much!

To each and every blogger who shares my teasers, excerpts, buy links, and anything else, THANK YOU! I admire and appreciate the work each of you do.

Readers, I'd be nowhere without you. Thank you for continuing to buy my books, thanks for the support, the love, and the kind words. I hope you keep sticking with me, because I have plenty more to come!

# BOOKS BY ISABEL LUCERO

The Secrets That We Keep
War

THE ESCORT SERIES
*Living in Sin (Escort 1)*
*Unforgivable Sin (Escort 2)*
*Sins & Mistrust (Escort 3)*

# ABOUT THE AUTHOR

ISABEL LUCERO IS THE AUTHOR of the romantic suspense novel The Secrets That We Keep and the best-selling erotic romance books Living in Sin, Unforgivable Sin, and Sins & Mistrust; books one, two, and three in The Escort Series.

She was born in a small town in New Mexico and was lucky enough to escape and travel the world thanks to her husband's career in the Air Force. She's been married for eleven years to the love of her life and Jr. High School sweetheart. Together they have two of the best and most beautiful kids in the world.

Isabel's love for reading is anything but new, she's been reading since before she was a teenager.

She's a multi-genre author, tackling genres such as romantic suspense, erotic romance, crime drama, and contemporary romance.

She currently lives overseas and is constantly coming up with new book ideas, so keep an eye open for new stories coming your way. Isabel loves connecting with her readers and fans of books in general. You can find her on her personal website, Facebook, Twitter, and Instagram.

*https://www.isabellucero.com*

*Turn the page for an excerpt from Defending Her by WS Greer*

# Defending Her

W.S. GREER

## CHAPTER 1

"HOW IS IT POSSIBLE FOR you to be that sexy?"

Valerie smiles at me in the mirror as I step out of the bathroom, just as she changes the channel on the TV. I feel a sharp tingle run up my back as I admire her sex appeal. I'm not really sure what it is, but there's just something about her that seems to always catch me off guard. She takes my breath away, and I find myself constantly having to snap out of it.

Every part of me lusts after her as I watch her turn around. Her blonde hair is perfectly curled at the ends, cascading over her petite, unbelievably sexy shoulder. She turns and faces me and we lock eyes. I let my gaze slowly scroll down her body as she shows herself to me—tempting me, teasing me.

"Can I admit something to you?" she says in a low, sultry tone.

"Of course," I reply, putting on my sexiest smirk.

"I've kind of been thinking about this all day." She reaches up and sweeps her bangs to the side, and then starts walking towards the bed. Her five-foot-five frame is perfectly put together, and I have to admit to myself that she has everything a man could ever want. Oh, the things I want to do to this woman.

"Oh yeah?" I answer. "Exactly which parts were you thinking about?"

I rest the back of my head on the headboard and watch as she slowly steps towards me. As she walks, I categorize her perfection. Hair, perfect. Face, stunning. Lips, luscious. Breasts, flawless. Hips, the sexiest, most perfect version of wide I've ever seen. Legs, breathtaking. I want her so bad I can feel it seeping from my pores.

Valerie finally makes it to the bed and stops only inches from me. She looks at me and I can see the desire in her eyes. She wants it just as much as I do. Then, without warning, she reaches up and pulls the straps to her dress off her shoulders and lets the garment drop down around her ankles. Her pale skin is radiant and I can't take my eyes off of her gorgeous body. Her green eyes pierce into me as she puts one knee on the mattress and pushes the covers back, exposing my naked body to the air. I don't shy away or cover myself up. Instead, I lay there confidently, welcoming her to climb on top of me and do whatever she wants. I lay there as she looks my body up and down with a grin spreading across her lips. This isn't the first time she's seen it, so she knows what to expect. She knows exactly what's about to happen.

"*This* is what I've been thinking about," she says as she reaches down and takes my hard cock in her hand and begins to massage it slowly. "I was thinking about how amazing it was the last time I was here. The last time I was in your house, and we were in this bedroom, on this bed. The way you made me feel. I kept smiling every time I thought about it. The other nurses were asking me what was making me smile so much, but it was my secret. My own little secret fantasy right there in the nurse's station. So, now that I'm here again, I want to feel it *again*."

The memory of how good it was the last time Valerie was here comes rushing back to me, and now I'm the one who has to force back a smile. It was two weeks ago, but I see the images in my head like it was just yesterday. We started on the floor of the bathroom, and then made our way to the floor in the bedroom. Then, I made her put her hands on the dresser so that she could watch us in the mirror as I thrust in and out of her from behind. We both had sweat dripping off our bodies, creating little puddles all over the dark hardwood floor. I remember the way her orgasm made her knees shake and buckle, and I had to hold her body so that she wouldn't completely collapse. Yes, I remember it all vividly, and I want it all again. I can't wait any longer.

I reach up and grab Valerie by her hips and force her on top of me. As she straddles me, she lets out an adorable giggle that makes my heart feel funny. I shake it off and focus on the sensation of her wetness resting on top of me. I can feel her clit pulsating as it sits on top of my shaft.

"So, you were thinking about me at work? Isn't that against the rules?" I say with a flirtatious grin.

Valerie moans as I force her hips forward and her clit rubs against my dick.

"I said I was thinking about *this.* I've been waiting for *this,*" she replies. "That's not against any rules, is it? I didn't say I missed you. I missed the way you make me feel."

"Mmhhm. Well, then I guess I should give you everything you've been waiting for. You ready for it?"

"Yes."

I reach down between her legs and rub her clit with my fingers. A smile takes over my face when I feel how wet she is. I move my fingers back and forth and revel in the sound of her moaning.

"Say it again," I continue. "Tell me you're ready for it."

"Yes, Jason. I'm ready for it. I'm ready."

"Good. Then, take it."

Valerie reaches down and takes ahold of my shaft,

and then slides me inside of her. I feel like my breath is sucked out of my lungs in a swoop. She feels *so* good.

She starts off slowly. Taking her time, methodically grinding her hips back and forth. Her blonde hair falls forward as she lowers her face to mine and kisses me softly, moaning into my mouth as I glide my tongue across hers. It's almost like we breathe in unison with each other as she begins to pick up speed, but she's careful not to go too fast. There's a part of me that wants to close my eyes, but if I did that, I wouldn't be able to see how sexy Valerie is. She has the kind of beauty that you don't want to miss, even for a second, so I keep my eyes open and watch her. Her eyes are closed and her hips move with a perfect rhythm. I watch her for a moment, but again, I make myself snap out of it. I know she's enjoying it, but I know how she *really* wants it.

"Is this what you were thinking about?" I ask, quietly.

Valerie doesn't open her eyes when she answers. "Yes," she says between deep breaths.

"Yeah? How about this?" All of a sudden, I lift my hand and smack her on the tiny spot between the top of her ass and the bottom of her back. I feel her jolt forward, and she lets out a blissful squeak.

"Yes!" she exclaims, but she still holds it back and it comes out almost like an exaggerated whisper. That won't cut it.

"Huh? Is this what you were missing?" I ask again, right before slapping her ass, this time with a force that stings my hand, so I know it was perfect.

"Yes! Yes, Jason!"

"Yeah? I want to hear you say it." I smack her again, this time with the other hand, on the other side of her ass.

"Yes! This is what I've been missing!"

I think about the last time she was here, and how strong her last orgasm was in front of that mirror on the dresser. I'm determined to outdo myself this time around.

See, a normal guy would just lay there and let her do all the work while he enjoys it. A normal guy is selfish. I, on the other hand, am *not* a normal guy. I'm not satisfied until she is. So, I grab ahold of Valerie's hips and take control of her. First, I take a tight grip on her hips and keep her from moving all together. She looks down at me in confusion at first, but when I look at her, she knows this isn't unintentional. I'm doing exactly what I want, which is exactly what *she* wants.

I begin to slowly force her hips back and forth, while making sure that I press her body down on mine so that her clit is constantly stimulated. I can hear her breathing starting to become harder for her to control, and her eyes close once again. She doesn't say anything, and that's exactly what I want now. I just want her to feel it. I want her to think about this every day until we meet up to do this again, no matter how long that takes.

I grip Valerie's hips even tighter, and force her to pick up speed, while I start to rotate my own hips so that she takes it deeper. I want her to feel all of me touching all of her. Her breathing is becoming even more unstable, and her excitement is starting to overwhelm her as she grips the covers next to my head and begins to moan louder. Luckily, the houses next to mine are at least twenty yards away, with thick, soundproof glass windows. So Valerie can let it all out, just like I want her to.

Valerie starts to move her body all on her own now. I find myself squeezing my eyes closed, overpowered by how good she feels. However, I don't just let her go. Even as Valerie starts to ride me so hard that the headboard is bouncing off the wall, I still manage to grind my hips with the same rhythm as her. She leans back and places both of her hands on my chest, and starts to ride me like a professional horse rider. Together, we push the frame of the bed away from the headboard, and it falls forward and lands on the mattress, just barely missing my head. But, we don't stop. Valerie continues to ride me, and I continue to throw it back to her from the bottom. I reach up and grab her pink, erect nipples with my finger tips and lightly squeeze them both.

"Yes, Jason! Yes!" Valerie screams as she lets her head fall backwards while she grinds on top of me. I smack her ass once again and she lets out a pleasure-filled scream that echoes off the walls and travels out the door and down the hallway. The bed continues to rock back and forth from the force of Valerie's thrusts, and I hear the comforter hit the floor as it falls off the bed, next to the pillow that fell off about ten seconds earlier. I squeeze one of her nipples once again while simultaneously smacking her ass with my other hand, then I see her skin on her chest and neck turn bright red. Her breathing sputters into short, staccato gasps, and then she inhales deeply before exploding into a guttural scream and falling forward onto me. She digs her nails into my chest as she climaxes, and I continue to grind my hips and push myself deeper into her. I wrap my arms around her body and lift my hips so high that it raises her body off the bed and she has to hold on to me for balance.

Finally, I feel the tension in her arms subside. Her muscles relax, and I hear her trying to catch her breath, but before she can, I roll my hips to the side and force both of us to roll over without having to pull out of her. The second we're repositioned, I start to thrust with long drawn out strokes.

"Oh my god, Jason!" she screams into my ear. I love

the way it sounds when she says my name, but I don't let it distract me. Instead, I place my left arm underneath Valerie's right knee and force her leg above my shoulder. I feel her foot dangling behind me as I force her to take it deep, and I plunge into her with powerful strokes.

"Yes, Jason. On my god, you're *so* good!" she bellows with her eyes cinched tight.

"Yeah. You like it deep?"

"Yes! Yes, I like it just like that!"

As I stroke in and out of her, I feel a strong sensation creeping its way forward. I try to slow down before it hits me, but Valerie just feels too good, and I'm suddenly overtaken by a massive orgasm. I bury my face in the pillow Valerie is laying on and scream into it as my body goes into involuntary convulsions. Valerie prolongs the feeling by arching her back and grinding her hips, completely taking my breath away. I literally struggle to breathe until my climax finally relinquishes and my body goes limp. I slowly pull myself out of her and fall down on the mattress that is now only half covered by sheets, and barely clinging to the box springs.

"Holy shit, that was good," I say, breathing heavily on my back as I slowly pull off the condom. "Is that what you were thinking about in the nurse's station?"

Valerie lets out an exhausted laugh as she stares up at the high ceiling. "Yeah, that was pretty much it. I'd say you hit the nail on the head."

"SO, A FULL TWO WEEKS went by this time. How come you took so long to call me? I was starting to think that you don't like spending time with me."

Valerie giggles to herself as she lays her head on my

bare stomach, staring up at the spinning fan on the ceiling. I've put my boxer briefs back on, but Valerie is still completely naked, using the comforter that we put back on the bed to cover her body.

"Yeah, right," she replies with a grin. "You know I love the time we spend together. Nothing brings me more pleasure than coming over here. I don't get relief like that *anywhere* else. Trust me."

"Okay then," I respond as I smile at the compliment. "Then what have you been up to that made you wait so long to come see me? I tried calling you, you know."

She seems to think to herself for a moment before she speaks again. It's something I've noticed about Valerie since I met her a little over five months ago. She's a thinker. Anytime I ask her something personal, she seems to always take a moment to think about her answer before she actually gives it. I'm not sure why that is, but I don't let myself become overly concerned about it. She's *not* my girlfriend, and she's allowed to do whatever she wants, and keep whatever secrets she wants. I don't have to know everything in her personal life. At least, that's what I tell myself.

"There wasn't anything in particular that kept me from calling. I've just been busy. I'm pulling double shifts at the hospital sometimes, so I just don't have a lot of time, but like I told you earlier, I still think about you. I mean, I think about what we do when we get together. I'm not forgetting about you."

"Then why don't you answer whenever I call you?"

Again, she takes a second to think about her answer. I force myself to wait patiently.

"You just seem to always call at the wrong time. A lot of times, I don't even have my phone with me because it can be a distraction at work. I can't be working with a patient or a doctor and be interrupted by my phone. I can't just drop what I'm doing. Then, by the time I get home, I'm just too tired. Don't take it personally though, Jason, I'm just really busy."

"I see." I reach down and push the covers off of her, exposing her breasts. Even in the dark, with nothing but the light of the TV shining, her body is exquisite. I feel like I can't even control myself as I reach down and begin to rub little circles around her nipples. I'm not really sure if it's to please her, or myself.

"What about you?" Valerie continues. "What have you been up to? Spending your time wooing any other nurses?"

I chuckle at the memory of how Valerie and I first met in the ER of Harborview Medical Center. I'd been hit in the head with a glass bottle at a bar in downtown Seattle, because some guy didn't like the idea of me talking to his woman when he had his back turned—go figure. My best friend, Jordan Harper, forced me to go to the ER because my head wouldn't stop bleeding. When I walked through the sliding doors, Valerie Benedict was sitting in the nurse's station. I don't know if it was from the concussion I was experiencing or not, but when I saw her, I felt dizzy. She was gorgeous. Those plump, pink lips and green eyes just knocked me off my feet, and I was immediately hooked. She was flawless, even in those ugly purple scrubs. Two days later, I went back to the ER just to see her again, but not in a stalker kind of way, or anything like that. She was just too beautiful to stay away from, even though I knew I wasn't interested in some serious, committed, exclusive relationship. I just wanted her. I had to have her.

"Well, I haven't been wooing any nurses, but I've been on some dates. I had one last weekend, actually," I reply, looking down at her, still circling my finger around her nipple.

"Oh really?"

"Yeah. Why? Does that bother you?"

She takes a second to think about it again. "No. No, of course not," she says, furrowing her brow and shaking her head for emphasis. "You're a grown man, Jason. You can do whatever you want to do. We both know what this is. You've got your life to live, and you're always busy with your job, just like I'm always busy with mine. I understand that being a lawyer is stressful and time consuming, just like being a nurse is. So, I'm doing what we said we'd do, and keeping the emotional side out of it. That's what we agreed."

"I know. What about you, though? You going on any dates? Any doctors or male nurse's trying to come sweep you off your feet?"

"No. I'm just too busy for anything like that. I don't pay attention to any of that stuff. No time."

"Yeah, but I know that you've got to have guys lining up at your door. I mean, look at you! There isn't a chance in hell that guys aren't noticing you."

"Well, that's sweet, but no. Nobody's hitting on me. At least not that I've noticed."

"Well, you must not be paying attention. Trust me, there are very few women in the *world* that look like you."

Valerie brushes her bangs away from her eyes and looks up at me. Our eye contact sends a bolt of lightning into my heart, and the smile that develops on her face makes me suddenly feel hot all over.

Just then, however, our connection is broken by the sound of her cell phone ringing in her purse on the dresser. We're both startled by the sound, but it seems to startle Valerie in a different way. Her eyes bulge at the noise and she suddenly jumps up, her calm demeanor suddenly replaced by a look of panic.

"Are you okay?" I ask, nervously.

Valerie gets up off the bed as fast as she can and stands there, looking around as if she doesn't know where the sound is coming from.

"Yeah. Umm, I'm fine. I just . . . umm," she stammers, almost incoherently.

"Val, what's the matter?" Her nervousness is actually beginning to make me feel anxious myself.

"Nothing. I just have to go. I have to go."

"What? Why?"

"It's uhh . . . because it's the hospital. I have to go," she replies as she bends over and picks up her dress off the floor and begins trying to straighten it out so she can put it back on.

"How do you know it's the hospital? You haven't even looked at your phone."

"I just know that it is, okay? I just have to go. I'm sorry. I uhh, I'm on standby."

"Alright," I reply as I start to get out of the bed so that I can at least walk her out.

"No, no. Don't get up. It's fine, I can see myself out. I'll call you later, okay?" Valerie finishes sliding into her dress, and quickly jumps into her high heels and snatches her purse off the dresser. Then, she comes over to the bed and gives me a quick, but passionate kiss on the lips that ends much too quickly. "I had a great time, as usual."

"Me too. I hope another two weeks doesn't go by before we see each other again. I'll call you. Maybe you'll actually answer this time."

"Maybe so. I'll talk to you later."

Just like that, Valerie turns on her heel and walks out of the room. I hear her heels clunking down the stairs as she speed walks over the hardwood floors, and races out the front door, slamming it closed behind her.

57735184R00155

Made in the USA
Charleston, SC
22 June 2016